# A SYNTAX-READER
# FOR THE GREEK NEW TESTAMENT

## *FIFTEEN LESSONS*

**James B. De Young**

*Wipf & Stock*
PUBLISHERS
*Eugene, Oregon*

Wipf and Stock Publishers
199 West 8th Avenue, Suite 3
Eugene, Oregon 97401

A Syntax-Reader for the Greek New Testament
Fifteen Lessons
By De Young, James B.
Copyright©2003 by De Young, James B.
ISBN: 978-1-4982-4714-6
Publication date 5/20/2004

# DEDICATION

I dedicate this *Syntax*-Reader first, to my many students, who over the years have encouraged me to pursue greater understanding of the Greek New Testament and the greater knowledge of God, and second, to my colleagues for their support in my teaching at Western Seminary.

# TABLE OF CONTENTS

# PREFACE

Many excellent texts on New Testament Greek grammar and syntax exist to lead students into deeper understanding of the language. Yet these approach the instruction of Greek in either a deductive or an inductive manner. The aim of this *Syntax-Reader* is to instruct students in the learning of Greek syntax by combining what the best texts contribute with a comprehensive reading of theologically significant passages of the New Testament. In this manner students come to appreciate the Greek for its own sake and, more importantly, as the foundation for exegesis and their understanding of theology and the truth of Scripture. By the end of the *Syntax-Reader* students will know not only Greek syntax but they will know how syntax contributes to translating and interpreting most of the passages which are basic to the doctrines of Christianity. By means of translation, questions for the "heart and mind," discussion questions, assignments, and syntactical charts, students advance from the doctrine of Scripture through the doctrines of God the Father, Christ the Son, the Holy Spirit, salvation, Satan, holiness, the Church, sin, the nature of people, spiritual gifts, justification by faith, the return of Christ, the exaltation of Christ, and union with Christ. In short, students learn theology as they learn Greek, and they learn Greek as they learn theology.

# ACKNOWLEDGMENTS

For the production of this book I wish to acknowledge the assistance of several people. These are my graduate fellows, Nancy Woods, Jason Johansen, and Justin Martz. Their contributions to the content of this book and its formatting have been helpful and creative.

The Greek text printed in this *Syntax Reader* is from *The Greek New Testament*, Fourth Revised Edition, edited by Barbara Aland, Kurt Aland, Johannes Karavidopoulos, Carlos M. Martini, and Bruce M. Metzger, in cooperation with the Institute for New Testament Textual Research, Munster/Westphalia. © 1993 Deutsche Bibelgesellschaft, Stuttgart. Used by permission.

# INTRODUCTION

The following pages present a unique approach to learning Greek syntax. In short, the goal is to learn advanced syntax, both deductively, by reading standard textbooks, and inductively, by reading the most theologically significant passages in the New Testament. The *Syntax-Reader* introduces students to all the literary genres of the New Testament while simultaneously acquainting them with the significant syntactical and exegetical issues involved in these texts.

## *THE APPROACH*

Each lesson of the *Syntax-Reader* has five sections.

(1) The first section presents the Greek text from three portions of the Greek New Testament. The order of these texts is always the same. First, a passage from John 14-17 is printed, then the accompanying texts from elsewhere in the New Testament. The Upper Room Discourse was selected as the starting point because it represents relatively easy Greek. The Discourse serves as a transition from an elementary knowledge of Greek to something more difficult. It is also a repository of ideas that form the basis of virtually all the doctrines of the Christian faith.

In each lesson the two additional passages that accompany the passage from John 14-17 treat the same topic or area of theology. These passages will lead the student through the whole spectrum of doctrines usually found in systematic theology. The goal is to enable students to become familiar with the most significant texts that they will encounter elsewhere in theological education (e.g., in classes of theology, church history, Biblical interpretation, preaching, Christian education, etc.).

The passages from John 14-17 average about 6-10 verses in length, and those from the other two passages about 10-12 verses in length (although shorter passages occur in the first lesson). The instructor may allow students to use any tools, including parsing guides, interlinears, and computer tools (*Bible Works*, *Logos*, *Gramcord*, etc.) to do their preparation of the translation of these passages before coming to class. Students should be encouraged to write out the translation between the printed lines of the text for recitation in class. The goal is not to do a lot of memory work, but to build word recognition and translation ability by constant repetition and exposure to the text.

(2) The second section consists of questions on the passages translated. These questions are designed for theological and devotional reflection. They appeal to the student's heart and mind. They are of a general nature and should arouse students' sense of the importance of the passages for the designated theological emphasis. Instructors may or may not require students to write out responses to these questions. In either case they become the basis for facilitating classroom discussion.

(3) The third section consists of questions framed for classroom discussion. The questions address the new points of syntax as they apply to the texts translated for that

particular lesson. The questions address issues of grammatical, exegetical, and theological importance. The instructor at his discretion may expand or abbreviate these questions.

(4) The fourth section of each lesson consists of a chart that outlines the new points of syntax for instruction, discussion and completion of the assignments. These charts are keyed to two texts widely used in New Testament syntax: James A. Brooks and Carlton L. Winbery, *Syntax of New Testament Greek* (Washington: University of America Press, 1979); and Daniel B. Wallace, *Greek Grammar Beyond the Basics* (Grand Rapids: Zondervan, 1996). I've derived the categories on the charts of this *Syntax-Reader* from these texts, and from several other middle-level and advanced grammars. The charts represent an easy way to access most aspects of syntax in the two grammars cited, since specific page numbers are listed in columns on the right. The first of these grammars follows the scheme of the eight-case system of the Greek noun, while the second grammar follows the scheme of the five case system. In this way students are introduced to both systems, and the charts are usable to everyone.

At the end of the *Syntax-Reader* all of the individual charts printed in each lesson are brought together in an appendix to provide a comprehensive listing of all the points of syntax. This feature provides a readily accessible resource for subsequent use (as in a course on exegesis).

(5) The final section consists of the homework assignments for each lesson. These assignments address points of syntax in the same theologically significant passages. The assignments are cumulative. Each lesson adds to the work previously learned. In this way students continue to advance in knowledge and understanding by repeated attention to the same points of grammar/syntax. For example, at the end of the course students must still identify the functions of noun cases, even though these are introduced at the beginning of the *Syntax-Reader*. The *Syntax-Reader* gives special attention to, and devotes more lessons to, the functions of noun cases and verb tenses. The instructor may require all or part of the requirements given on these pages.

The approach of this *Syntax-Reader* is both deductive and inductive. It is deductive in that students study one or two texts on syntax. These books, along with the contents of several other major works on Greek syntax, are summarized by the charts of each lesson. Students use these charts to do their written assignments. The approach of the *Syntax-Reader* is also inductive in that students translate for each lesson approximately thirty verses drawn from three passages. This amount of reading promotes the learning of vocabulary, grammar, and syntax by exposure and repetition. The deductive and inductive approaches come together as students seek to apply the categories of the functions of syntax to the passages being translated. Homework and in-class discussion reinforce each other to develop the skills of students for translating and doing syntax. The five parts of each lesson reinforce each other.

This *Syntax-Reader* with its fifteen lessons is planned for a term of fifteen weeks. A class that meets twice a week for a total of three to four hours per week (earning three or four credit hours) should be able to complete the text in this allotted time. At the instructor's discretion, combining a couple of them into one could reduce the number of lessons. While I've written the *Syntax-Reader* for classroom usage, it is possible to suit the text to distance learning and independent learning. It could be computerized. Midterm and final exams should be created and given at the instructor's discretion.

## *PROCEDURE*

In my experience in teaching the approach of the *Syntax-Reader*, I've used class time in the following way. The four-hour class meets twice a week for two hours each time. At the beginning of the first two-hour session, one of the students is selected to read a devotional entry that all of the students are required to record in a journal each week. This exercise is the student's reflection on one of the three passages being translated for that week.

After prayer, students read their translations that they have written out between the lines of the printed texts found at the beginning of each lesson. Then the questions from the section, "Questions for Heart and Mind," are discussed. This activity allows students to begin interpreting the passages to develop their theological understanding.

Once or twice during the term I have found it helpful to have students participate in a case study that involves the theological importance of the syntax being discussed. For example, after students have translated the passages on Christology, including Colossians 1:15-20, they assume the various roles of the participants of the Council of Nicea and its debate over the nature of Christ. The personages, beliefs, conflicts, and resolution of the Council are role played and discussed. In this way students see the significant way that the syntax of Colossians 1:16, in particular, and other passages, has impacted the theology of the Church, and continues to do so by the various modern counterparts to ancient Arianism. A helpful resource is Jack Rogers, *et al*, *Case Studies in Christ and Salvation* (Philadelphia: The Westminster Press, 1977).

Before returning for the second class session of two hours, students are required to complete the homework sheets assigned the previous week and to read about the new syntax topic designated for the day. At the start of class, another student reads a devotional entry and prayer is shared. Then students report and grade their homework while the instructor designates what the correct answers are. In this manner students immediately know how they have grasped the points of syntax and are encouraged to ask questions to clarify why their answers are correct or incorrect. In other words, students grade all their homework in class with the instructor providing the correct answers. Often two or more answers are possible as acceptable options.

Then the instructor teaches the new topic of syntax designated on the syllabus and in the table of contents. As the instructor teaches, the students follow the charts summarizing the new syntax for the new lesson. This step involves discussion of the points of syntax by utilizing the references listed on the charts for each category. Following this step, the instructor appoints one of the students to lead the discussion of the "Class Discussion Questions." This activity encourages students to participate freely in the discussion. The questions of this section are oriented toward utilizing and reinforcing the new points of syntax, and to show again their relevance for exegesis, theology, and living. The period concludes with the instructor's assigning the amount of homework to do for the particular lesson.

Students do all their homework on passages only after first translating them earlier in the week at the first session and after instruction on the new aspects of syntax. Also at this time the instructor assigns the new passages to be translated for the next session.

In summary, the homework for each week consists of the translation of the new passages for the first session, then for the second session the completion of written assignments that require students to decipher the syntax from the passages translated during the first session a week earlier. Students use the categories listed on the summary charts. Each week the first session is devoted to translation and initial devotional-theological observation while the second session is devoted to identifying the functions of the syntax.

Each new lesson of homework incorporates the syntax previously taught. Thus on the major sections of syntax (noun cases, verb tenses) there is a gradual accumulation of more and more syntax repeatedly utilized in subsequent lessons.

The approach of this *Syntax-Reader* gives students multiple exposures both to the Greek passages and to the new and accumulated syntax. Learning from one week to the next reinforces the previous learning.

## *ADVANTAGES OF THIS APPROACH*

There are several advantages to this *Syntax-Reader* and its approach. First of all, it is a programmed and graded reader. Each lesson of the *Syntax-Reader* has a deliberate arrangement so that easier portions occur before more difficult readings. In several cases, progressively more difficult passages occur as one moves to successive lessons. The *Syntax-Reader* emphasizes the more important parts of the sentence and of syntax by giving special attention and repeated review to the functions of the cases of the noun and to the tenses of the verb. Yet all points of syntax are covered by the lessons.

This *Syntax-Reader* effectively combines the better elements of an inductive and a deductive approach to learning biblical Greek. It builds upon an elementary foundation of Greek grammar. Once finished this text lays a good foundation for a course in exegesis.

This approach also leads students to the direct use of their Greek ability to translate and to understand what they are reading. By using theologically significant texts it is highly probable that students will study these very texts in their other classes in Bible college or seminary. This inter-disciplinary feature will give students the advantage of being acquainted with the Greek text of the most important doctrinal passages of the New Testament. Students begin building a Biblical theology in their Greek classes.

The points of grammar and syntax are repeatedly emphasized—by the translation of the Scripture, by the instruction in class, by the class assignments for class discussion, by the homework assignments, and even by the devotional journal entries (which are optional). Students learn by repeated exposure to a growing base of material.

The *Syntax-Reader* is also flexible.    Instructors can alter the assignments in various ways.  They can decide how to hold students accountable for the reading, how much of the written assignments to require, and make other adjustments relative to their vision for the course and the needs of students.

A word of explanation is in order regarding the charts in the appendix.  These charts are meant to be "Quick Reference Guides," and do not supplant the reading of either or both of the texts (as the instructor may determine).  The categories reflect the author's own judgment.  In some cases the categories depart from terminology used in the texts, or the number of categories may not correspond with the number delineated in the texts.  The instructor and the students can make adjustments as they wish.  May God use this work to advance his kingdom on the earth.

Summer, 2004.

# LESSON ONE:
# SYMBOLISM ABOUT TRUTH/WORD

## Lamp

### Book

A book most commonly represents the Word of God, the Bible. An open book represents truth or revelation. A closed book may be presumed to contain the names of the elect, and so may symbolize the Last Judgment and the inheritance of the saints. In the hands of an Apostle, a book represents the writings of the New Testament (Old Testament writings are usually represented by a scroll). A book is used in the emblems of many saints, among them John the Baptist, Stephen, Bartholomew, Matthias and Simon.

The lamp is most often used to represent the Word of God. It may also be used as a symbol of wisdom taken from the parable of the wise and foolish virgins in Matthew 25. The lamp was associated in the Old Testament with worship, where it symbolized God's presence. A lamp can also represent life itself, or the Holy Spirit's indwelling. An interesting use of the word "lamp" in the Old Testament comes from several references to God's promise to preserve King David's descendants ("maintain a lamp"). It is also an emblem of several saints. The lamp is sometimes portrayed as an oil lamp more common in the land of Israel.

Text and images of the symbols come from http://www.bright.net; or home.att.net/~wegast/symbols/symbols.htm, Walter E. Gast, author and artist.

## READING ABOUT TRUTH/THE WORD

**John 14:1** Μὴ ταρασσέσθω ὑμῶν ἡ καρδία· πιστεύετε εἰς τὸν θεὸν καὶ εἰς ἐμὲ

πιστεύετε. **2** ἐν τῇ οἰκίᾳ τοῦ πατρός μου μοναὶ πολλαί εἰσιν· εἰ δὲ μή, εἶπον ἂν ὑμῖν

ὅτι πορεύομαι ἑτοιμάσαι τόπον ὑμῖν; **3** καὶ ἐὰν πορευθῶ καὶ ἑτοιμάσω τόπον ὑμῖν,

πάλιν ἔρχομαι καὶ παραλήμψομαι ὑμᾶς πρὸς ἐμαυτόν, ἵνα ὅπου εἰμὶ ἐγὼ καὶ ὑμεῖς ἦτε.

**4** καὶ ὅπου [ἐγὼ] ὑπάγω οἴδατε τὴν ὁδόν. **5** Λέγει αὐτῷ Θωμᾶς· κύριε, οὐκ οἴδαμεν

ποῦ ὑπάγεις· πῶς δυνάμεθα τὴν ὁδὸν εἰδέναι; **6** λέγει αὐτῷ [ὁ] Ἰησοῦς· ἐγώ εἰμι ἡ

ὁδὸς καὶ ἡ ἀλήθεια καὶ ἡ ζωή· οὐδεὶς ἔρχεται πρὸς τὸν πατέρα εἰ μὴ δι' ἐμοῦ. **7** εἰ

ἐγνώκατέ με, καὶ τὸν πατέρα μου γνώσεσθε. καὶ ἀπ' ἄρτι γινώσκετε αὐτὸν καὶ

ἑωράκατε αὐτόν.

**Matthew 5:17** Μὴ νομίσητε ὅτι ἦλθον καταλῦσαι τὸν νόμον ἢ τοὺς προφήτας· οὐκ

ἦλθον καταλῦσαι ἀλλὰ πληρῶσαι. **18** ἀμὴν γὰρ λέγω ὑμῖν· ἕως ἂν παρέλθῃ ὁ οὐρανὸς

καὶ ἡ γῆ, ἰῶτα ἓν ἢ μία κεραία οὐ μὴ παρέλθῃ ἀπὸ τοῦ νόμου, ἕως ἂν πάντα γένηται.

**19** ὃς ἐὰν οὖν λύσῃ μίαν τῶν ἐντολῶν τούτων τῶν ἐλαχίστων καὶ διδάξῃ οὕτως τοὺς

ἀνθρώπους, ἐλάχιστος κληθήσεται ἐν τῇ βασιλείᾳ τῶν οὐρανῶν· ὃς δ' ἂν ποιήσῃ καὶ

διδάξῃ, οὗτος μέγας κληθήσεται ἐν τῇ βασιλείᾳ τῶν οὐρανῶν. **20** Λέγω γὰρ ὑμῖν ὅτι ἐὰν μὴ περισσεύσῃ ὑμῶν ἡ δικαιοσύνη πλεῖον τῶν γραμματέων καὶ Φαρισαίων, οὐ μὴ

εἰσέλθητε εἰς τὴν βασιλείαν τῶν οὐρανῶν.

**2 Timothy 3:14** Σὺ δὲ μένε ἐν οἷς ἔμαθες καὶ ἐπιστώθης, εἰδὼς παρὰ τίνων ἔμαθες,

**15** καὶ ὅτι ἀπὸ βρέφους [τὰ] ἱερὰ γράμματα οἶδας, τὰ δυνάμενά σε σοφίσαι εἰς

σωτηρίαν διὰ πίστεως τῆς ἐν Χριστῷ Ἰησοῦ. **16** πᾶσα γραφὴ θεόπνευστος καὶ

ὠφέλιμος πρὸς διδασκαλίαν, πρὸς ἐλεγμόν, πρὸς ἐπανόρθωσιν, πρὸς παιδείαν τὴν ἐν

δικαιοσύνῃ, **17** ἵνα ἄρτιος ᾖ ὁ τοῦ θεοῦ ἄνθρωπος, πρὸς πᾶν ἔργον ἀγαθὸν

ἐξηρτισμένος.

**2 Peter 1:19** καὶ ἔχομεν βεβαιότερον τὸν προφητικὸν λόγον, ᾧ καλῶς ποιεῖτε

προσέχοντες ὡς λύχνῳ φαίνοντι ἐν αὐχμηρῷ τόπῳ, ἕως οὗ ἡμέρα διαυγάσῃ καὶ

φωσφόρος ἀνατείλῃ ἐν ταῖς καρδίαις ὑμῶν, **20** τοῦτο πρῶτον γινώσκοντες ὅτι πᾶσα

προφητεία γραφῆς ἰδίας ἐπιλύσεως οὐ γίνεται· **21** οὐ γὰρ θελήματι ἀνθρώπου ἠνέχθη

προφητεία ποτέ, ἀλλὰ ὑπὸ πνεύματος ἁγίου φερόμενοι ἐλάλησαν ἀπὸ θεοῦ ἄνθρωποι.

# QUESTIONS FOR HEART AND MIND

## TRUTH/WORD

### MATTHEW 5:17-20; 2 TIMOTHY 3:14-17; 2 PETER 1:19-21

1. To what extent is the law secure (Matt. 5:17-20)?


   How does verse 17 impact the relationship of the Testaments?


2. What is the meaning of Jesus' reference to the "iota" and "horn"? Is he referring only to the letters on the page?


3. a. To what does "Scripture" refer in 2 Timothy 3:16?

   b. To what does "prophecy" refer in 2 Peter 1:20ff.?

   c. What are the implications for our use of translations?  For our use of the OT?


4. Compare the NASB translation of 2 Timothy 3:16 with the marginal note.  How may the difference affect our understanding of the nature of Scripture?


5. In view of these three passages, what is the nature of Scripture and the scope of its "profitability"?  What is inspired?


6. How is the prophetic word "more sure" (2 Pet. 1:19)?


   How does the answer reflect the relation of revelation to experience?


7. How do the meanings of ἰδίας and ἐπιλύσεως affect the interpretation of 2 Peter 1:20-21? Is the passage speaking of interpretation or origination?

# SYNTAX

## CASES

| Function | Key Concepts | N.T. Example | *B&W | **Wall |
|---|---|---|---|---|
| **A. NOMINATIVE (Designation)** | | | | |
| 1. Subject Nom. | Usual Subject | Jn.1:5; 3:35 | 3 | 38 |
| 2. Predicate Nom. | Appositional/ linking verb | 1 Jn.4:8; Jn.1:14 | 4 | 40 |
| 3. Nom. Of Appelation | Used as Proper Noun | Jn.13:13; Rev.1:4 | 5 | 61 |
| 4. Independent Nom. | Absolute (salutations, titles; no sentence) | Mk.1:1, 3; Mt.1:1; Rev.1:1; Rom.1:7 | 5 | 49 |
| 5. Nom. Of Exclamation | "Brothers!" | Mk.3:34; Rom.11:33 | 7 | 59 |
| 6. Pendent | Logical, not gram. subj. | Jn.1:12; Rev.3:12 | -- | 51 |
| 7. Apposition | Identity ("namely") | Lk.1:13; Rom.1:1 | 7 | 48 |
| **B. VOCATIVE (Address)** | | | | |
| 1. Direct Address | Isolated Word | Jn.6:68; Lk.1:3 | 64 | 65 |
| 2. Apposition | Identity ("namely") | Mk.5:7; Ac.13:10 | -- | 70 |

## CLASS DISCUSSION QUESTIONS

### NOMINATIVE AND VOCATIVE CASES

### TRUTH/WORD

### MATTHEW 5:17-20; 2 TIMOTHY 3:14-17; 2 PETER 1:19-21

1. Compare the NASB translation of 2 Timothy 3:16 with the marginal note or NRSV. If the copula εστιν is supplied before θεόπνευστος (between γραφὴ and θεόπνευστος), what use of the nominative, θεόπνευστος, is involved? What is the translation?

   If the copula εστιν is put after καὶ and before ὠφέλιμος what is the use of the nominative?

   What is the translation?

   What are the implications for each view?

   What is meant by γραφὴ ? What are the implications?

   How do verses 16 and 17 relate to the spiritual disciplines?

2. To what do the words, ἰῶτα "smallest letter" and κεραία "stroke" (5:18, NASV), refer?

   What are the implications for possible views of Scripture?

   How does this impact translation?

# ASSIGNMENT

## IDENTIFY SYNTACTICAL FUNCTIONS: CASES

## NOMINATIVE AND VOCATIVE

## MATTHEW 5:17-20; 2 TIMOTHY 3:14-17; 2 PETER 1:19-21

Identify the case and its function
*Matthew 5:17-20*

1. οὐρανὸς (v. 18)

2. ἰῶτα

3. πάντα

4. ἐλάχιστος (v. 19)

5. οὗτος

6. μέγας

7. δικαιοσύνη (v. 20)

*2 Timothy 3:14-17*

1. Σὺ (v. 14)

2. γραφὴ (v. 16)

3. θεόπνευστος

4. ὠφέλιμος

5. ἄρτιος (v. 17)

6. ἄνθρωπος

7. ἐξηρτισμένος

*2 Peter 1:19-21*

1. ἡμέρα (v. 19)

2. φωσφόρος

3. προφητεία (v. 20)

4. ἄνθρωποι (v. 21)

BLANK

# LESSON TWO:
# SYMBOLISM ABOUT GOD/FATHER

## Hand (*Manus Dei*)

The hand of God (Manus Dei) is used as a symbol of God the Father. It was virtually the only symbol for God used during the first eight centuries of the church. The hand symbolizes God's ownership of and providence for all of creation, and comes from the many references to the "hand of God" in the Bible. The Manus Dei may take other forms. A hand clutching five persons indicates God's care and concern for people. A hand with the thumb, index and middle fingers extended with the others folded back on the palm is a Latin form symbolic of the Trinity. A hand with index finger extended, middle finger curled to form a "C", thumb crossed over the ring finger and little finger curled into another "C" forms the letters IX XC, an abbreviation for the Greek name of Jesus Christ.

# LESSON TWO

## READING ABOUT GOD/FATHER

**John 14:8** Λέγει αὐτῷ Φίλιππος· κύριε, δεῖξον ἡμῖν τὸν πατέρα, καὶ ἀρκεῖ ἡμῖν. **9**

λέγει αὐτῷ ὁ Ἰησοῦς· τοσούτῳ χρόνῳ μεθ᾽ ὑμῶν εἰμι καὶ οὐκ ἔγνωκάς με, Φίλιππε; ὁ

ἑωρακὼς ἐμὲ ἑώρακεν τὸν πατέρα· πῶς σὺ λέγεις· δεῖξον ἡμῖν τὸν πατέρα; **10** οὐ

πιστεύεις ὅτι ἐγὼ ἐν τῷ πατρὶ καὶ ὁ πατὴρ ἐν ἐμοί ἐστιν; τὰ ῥήματα ἃ ἐγὼ λέγω ὑμῖν

ἀπ᾽ ἐμαυτοῦ οὐ λαλῶ, ὁ δὲ πατὴρ ἐν ἐμοὶ μένων ποιεῖ τὰ ἔργα αὐτοῦ. **11** πιστεύετέ μοι

ὅτι ἐγὼ ἐν τῷ πατρὶ καὶ ὁ πατὴρ ἐν ἐμοί· εἰ δὲ μή, διὰ τὰ ἔργα αὐτὰ πιστεύετε. **12**

Ἀμὴν ἀμὴν λέγω ὑμῖν, ὁ πιστεύων εἰς ἐμὲ τὰ ἔργα ἃ ἐγὼ ποιῶ κἀκεῖνος ποιήσει καὶ

μείζονα τούτων ποιήσει, ὅτι ἐγὼ πρὸς τὸν πατέρα πορεύομαι· **13** καὶ ὅ τι ἂν αἰτήσητε

ἐν τῷ ὀνόματί μου τοῦτο ποιήσω, ἵνα δοξασθῇ ὁ πατὴρ ἐν τῷ υἱῷ. **14** ἐάν τι αἰτήσητέ

με ἐν τῷ ὀνόματί μου ἐγὼ ποιήσω. **15** Ἐὰν ἀγαπᾶτέ με, τὰς ἐντολὰς τὰς ἐμὰς

τηρήσετε·

**Acts 17:22** Σταθεὶς δὲ [ὁ] Παῦλος ἐν μέσῳ τοῦ Ἀρείου πάγου ἔφη· ἄνδρες Ἀθηναῖοι,

κατὰ πάντα ὡς δεισιδαιμονεστέρους ὑμᾶς θεωρῶ. **23** διερχόμενος γὰρ καὶ ἀναθεωρῶν

τὰ σεβάσματα ὑμῶν εὗρον καὶ βωμὸν ἐν ᾧ ἐπεγέγραπτο· Ἀγνώστῳ θεῷ. ὃ οὖν

ἀγνοοῦντες εὐσεβεῖτε, τοῦτο ἐγὼ καταγγέλλω ὑμῖν. **24** ὁ θεὸς ὁ ποιήσας τὸν κόσμον

καὶ πάντα τὰ ἐν αὐτῷ, οὗτος οὐρανοῦ καὶ γῆς ὑπάρχων κύριος οὐκ ἐν χειροποιήτοις

ναοῖς κατοικεῖ **25** οὐδὲ ὑπὸ χειρῶν ἀνθρωπίνων θεραπεύεται προσδεόμενός τινος,

αὐτὸς διδοὺς πᾶσι ζωὴν καὶ πνοὴν καὶ τὰ πάντα· **26** ἐποίησέν τε ἐξ ἑνὸς πᾶν ἔθνος

ἀνθρώπων κατοικεῖν ἐπὶ παντὸς προσώπου τῆς γῆς, ὁρίσας προστεταγμένους καιροὺς

καὶ τὰς ὁροθεσίας τῆς κατοικίας αὐτῶν **27** ζητεῖν τὸν θεόν, εἰ ἄρα γε ψηλαφήσειαν

αὐτὸν καὶ εὕροιεν, καί γε οὐ μακρὰν ἀπὸ ἑνὸς ἑκάστου ἡμῶν ὑπάρχοντα. **28** ἐν αὐτῷ

γὰρ ζῶμεν καὶ κινούμεθα καὶ ἐσμέν, ὡς καί τινες τῶν καθ᾽ ὑμᾶς ποιητῶν εἰρήκασιν·

τοῦ γὰρ καὶ γένος ἐσμέν. **29** γένος οὖν ὑπάρχοντες τοῦ θεοῦ οὐκ ὀφείλομεν νομίζειν

χρυσῷ ἢ ἀργύρῳ ἢ λίθῳ, χαράγματι τέχνης καὶ ἐνθυμήσεως ἀνθρώπου, τὸ θεῖον εἶναι

ὅμοιον. **30** τοὺς μὲν οὖν χρόνους τῆς ἀγνοίας ὑπεριδὼν ὁ θεός, τὰ νῦν παραγγέλλει τοῖς ἀνθρώποις πάντας πανταχοῦ μετανοεῖν, 31 καθότι ἔστησεν ἡμέραν ἐν ᾗ μέλλει κρίνειν τὴν οἰκουμένην ἐν δικαιοσύνῃ, ἐν ἀνδρὶ ᾧ ὥρισεν, πίστιν παρασχὼν πᾶσιν ἀναστήσας αὐτὸν ἐκ νεκρῶν.

**James 1:12** Μακάριος ἀνὴρ ὃς ὑπομένει πειρασμόν, ὅτι δόκιμος γενόμενος λήμψεται τὸν στέφανον τῆς ζωῆς ὃν ἐπηγγείλατο τοῖς ἀγαπῶσιν αὐτόν. 13 Μηδεὶς πειραζόμενος λεγέτω ὅτι ἀπὸ θεοῦ πειράζομαι· ὁ γὰρ θεὸς ἀπείραστός ἐστιν κακῶν, πειράζει δὲ αὐτὸς οὐδένα. 14 ἕκαστος δὲ πειράζεται ὑπὸ τῆς ἰδίας ἐπιθυμίας ἐξελκόμενος καὶ δελεαζόμενος· 15 εἶτα ἡ ἐπιθυμία συλλαβοῦσα τίκτει ἁμαρτίαν, ἡ δὲ ἁμαρτία ἀποτελεσθεῖσα ἀποκύει θάνατον. 16 Μὴ πλανᾶσθε, ἀδελφοί μου ἀγαπητοί. 17 πᾶσα δόσις ἀγαθὴ καὶ πᾶν δώρημα τέλειον ἄνωθέν ἐστιν καταβαῖνον ἀπὸ τοῦ πατρὸς τῶν φώτων, παρ' ᾧ οὐκ ἔνι παραλλαγὴ ἢ τροπῆς ἀποσκίασμα. 18 βουληθεὶς ἀπεκύησεν ἡμᾶς λόγῳ ἀληθείας εἰς τὸ εἶναι ἡμᾶς ἀπαρχήν τινα τῶν αὐτοῦ κτισμάτων.

# QUESTIONS FOR HEART AND MIND

## GOD/FATHER

### ACTS 17:22-31

1.  List seven attributes of God derived from this passage.

2.  How does verse 28 impact the idea of the "inspiration" of Scripture and other literature?

3.  What other Pauline passages are similar to verses 29-30?

4.  What is the significance of the resurrection (v. 32)? Note the presence of πίστιν.

5.  How would you summarize the three responses (vv. 32-34) to Paul's words?

6.  Is Paul's approach here a model for us to follow today? That is, if Paul adapts his message to the worldview of the Epicureans and Stoics (17:18, 28), what does this suggest to us living during the rise of a postmodern worldview?

# QUESTIONS FOR HEART AND MIND

## GOD/FATHER

### JAMES 1:12-18

1. List five characteristics of the nature of God from this passage.

2. For what reasons may we not say, "I am tempted by God"?

3. What is the double meaning of πειρασμός in this passage?  How can we discern the difference?

4. What is the difference between δόσις and δώρημα ?

5. How does verse 18 relate to verse 15?

6. What is the source of temptation for us according to this passage? What other sources are there?

# CLASS DISCUSSION QUESTIONS

## NOMINATIVE, VOCATIVE, GENITIVE CASES

## GOD/FATHER

## ACTS 17:22-31

1.    What is the use of ἄνδρες (v. 22)? Ἀθηναῖοι (v. 22)?


Does the second term inform us of the gender of the first?


How does the context help to answer the question (v. 34)?


What are the implications for translating ἄνδρες elsewhere (cf. Acts 2:14, etc.)?


2.    What are the possibilities for the gen. οὐρανοῦ καὶ γῆς (v. 24)?



What are the implications/applications for Christian living, faith and world view?



3.    What are the possibilities for the genitive γένος (οὖν ὑπάρχοντες) τοῦ θεοῦ (v. 29)?

What are the theological implications?

# CLASS DISCUSSION QUESTIONS

## NOMINATIVE, VOCATIVE, GENITIVE CASES

## GOD/FATHER

## JAMES 1:12-18

1.    What are the possible functions of the genitive ζωῆς (1:12)?

      What are the theological significances in each case?

2.    With the passive verb what preposition might have been expected with θεοῦ (1:13; cf. v. 14)?

      What is the theological difference between the use of ὑπὸ and ἀπὸ ?

      What may have been James' reason for his choice of preposition?

      What may we affirm as to the source or cause of temptation (1:14)?

      How does the denial of the source of temptation affect the meaning of πειραζομαι (cf. v. 12, πειρασμόν)?

      What else in the verse confirms this?

3.    What are the possibilities for the genitive φώτων (1:17)?

      What are the implications of each?

4.    What are the possible uses for the genitive ἀληθείας (1:18)?

      What are the implications of each?

# SYNTAX

# CASES

**GENITIVE (Description)**

| | | | | |
|---|---|---|---|---|
| 1. Description | Characterized, described by | Mk.1:4; Jn.2:16; Rom.13:12 | 8 | 79 |
| | Attributed/Attributive | Rom.6:4/6:6; Heb.3:12 | -- | 86, 89 |
| 2. Possession | Ownership/ Belonging to | Mt.26:51; Jn.1:12 | 8 | 81 |
| 3. Relationship | Familial/Marital | Mt.4:21; Jn.6:71 | 9 | 83 |
| 4. Adverbial | Adverb | | | |
| a. of time | kind of time | Mt.24:20; Jn.3:2 | 10 | 122 |
| b. of measure | price, value, quantity | Mt.10:29; Ju.11 | 11 | 122 |
| c. of place | where | Lk.19:4; 1 Pet.1:1 | 12 | 124 |
| d. of reference | "with reference to" | Heb.5:13; Jas.1:13 | 14 | 127 |
| e. of association | "with"(συν) | Rom.8:17; Mt.23:30 | -- | 128 |
| 5. Producer/Product | Genitive produces/is product | Eph.4:3; Phil.4:7/Rom.15:13,33 | -- | 104, 6 |
| 6. With Nouns of Action | | | | |
| a. Subjective | gen. produces act. | Rom.8:35; 16:25 | 15 | 113 |
| b. Objective | gen. receives act. | 1 Cor.1:6; Mt.12:31 | 15 | 116 |
| c. Plenary | both sub and obj | 2 Cor.5:14? Rev.1:1? | -- | 119 |
| 7. Partitive | Whole of which a part | Rev.8:7; Mk.6:23; Col.1:15? | 30 | 84 |
| 8. Apposition (in, of) | Identity; content; definition; material ("namely") | Rom.4:11; Jn.2:21 | 16 | 95 |
| 9. Absolute | Grammatically unconnected | Mt.2:1; Mk.9:28 | 17 | 127 |
| 10. Advantage,Purpose,Destiny | On behalf of; for | Col.4:3; Ac.4:9; Gal. 2:7 | 18 | 100 |
| 11. Subordination | Dominion ("over") | Mt.9:34; Mk.15:32 | -- | 103 |
| 12. Direct Object | With verbs of sense, emotion, sharing, desiring, ruling, buying, accusing | Lk.15:25; Heb.2:14 | 20 | 131 |
| 13. With Adjs. Advs. Nouns | Completes sense | Rom.1:32; Phil.1:27; Mt.26:66 | -- | 134 |
| 14. With Prepositions | δια, επι, κατα, μετα, περι, προς, υπερ | | 60-62 | 136 |

# ASSIGNMENT

## IDENTIFY SYNTACTICAL FORMS/FUNCTIONS:  CASES

## NOMINATIVE, VOCATIVE, GENITIVE.

## ACTS 17:22-31

Identify the case and its function

1. Παῦλος (v. 22)

2. ʼΑρείου πάγου

3. ἄνδρες

4. ʼΑθηναῖοι

5. ὑμῶν (v. 23)

6. κύριος (v. 24)

7. οὐρανοῦ

8. ἀνθρωπίνων (v. 25)

9. ἀνθρώπων (v. 26)

10. γῆς

11. κατοικίας

12. ἡμῶν (v. 27)

13. ποιητῶν (v. 28)

14. γένος

15. τοῦ

16. θεοῦ (v. 29)

17. τέχνης

18. ἐνθυμήσεως

19. ἀνθρώπου

20. ἀγνοίας (v. 30)

# ASSIGNMENT

## IDENTIFY SYNTACTICAL FORMS/FUNCTIONS:  CASES

## NOMINATIVE, VOCATIVE, GENITIVE

## JAMES 1:12-18

Identify the case and its function

1. ἀνὴρ  (v. 12)

2. δόκιμος

3. ζωῆς

4. Μηδεὶς  (v. 13)

5. ἀπείραστός

6. ἰδίας  (v. 14)

7. ἐπιθυμία  (v. 15)

8. ἀδελφοί  (v. 16)

9. δόσις  (v. 17)

10. φώτων

11. παραλλαγὴ

12. τροπῆς

13. κτισμάτων  (v. 18)

14. αὐτοῦ

15. ἀληθείας

# LESSON THREE:
# SYMBOLISM ABOUT CHRIST/SON

## Alpha and Omega

Alpha and omega are the first and last letters of the Greek alphabet, and thus refer to the eternal nature of Christ.

Rev. 1:8 "I am the Alpha and the Omega," says the Lord God, "who is, and who was, and who is to come, the Almighty." *(NIV)*

## Fish

The initial letters of the Greek phrase "Jesus Christ, Son of God, Savior" form the Greek word ICHTHUS, which means "fish." This symbol was used by believers in the early days of persecution as a secret sign of their shared faith. One person would draw an arc in the sand, and the other would complete the sign to show his brotherhood in Christ.

## Candle

A candle calls to mind Jesus' words, "I am the Light of the World" (John 8:12). When two candles are placed on an altar, they represent Jesus' human and divine natures. Believers are also called to be the light of the world:

## Violet

The violet is a symbol of humility. It is most often used in reference to the Virgin Mary, or to Christ's assuming human form.

# LESSON THREE

## READING ABOUT CHRIST/SON

**John 14:16** κἀγὼ ἐρωτήσω τὸν πατέρα καὶ ἄλλον παράκλητον δώσει ὑμῖν, ἵνα μεθ᾽

ὑμῶν εἰς τὸν αἰῶνα ᾖ, **17** τὸ πνεῦμα τῆς ἀληθείας, ὃ ὁ κόσμος οὐ δύναται λαβεῖν, ὅτι

οὐ θεωρεῖ αὐτὸ οὐδὲ γινώσκει· ὑμεῖς γινώσκετε αὐτό, ὅτι παρ᾽ ὑμῖν μένει καὶ ἐν ὑμῖν

ἔσται. **18** Οὐκ ἀφήσω ὑμᾶς ὀρφανούς, ἔρχομαι πρὸς ὑμᾶς. **19** ἔτι μικρὸν καὶ ὁ κόσμος

με οὐκέτι θεωρεῖ, ὑμεῖς δὲ θεωρεῖτέ με, ὅτι ἐγὼ ζῶ καὶ ὑμεῖς ζήσετε. **20** ἐν ἐκείνῃ τῇ

ἡμέρᾳ γνώσεσθε ὑμεῖς ὅτι ἐγὼ ἐν τῷ πατρί μου καὶ ὑμεῖς ἐν ἐμοὶ κἀγὼ ἐν ὑμῖν. **21** ὁ

ἔχων τὰς ἐντολάς μου καὶ τηρῶν αὐτὰς ἐκεῖνός ἐστιν ὁ ἀγαπῶν με· ὁ δὲ ἀγαπῶν με

ἀγαπηθήσεται ὑπὸ τοῦ πατρός μου, κἀγὼ ἀγαπήσω αὐτὸν καὶ ἐμφανίσω αὐτῷ ἐμαυτόν.

**22** Λέγει αὐτῷ Ἰούδας, οὐχ ὁ Ἰσκαριώτης· κύριε, [καὶ] τί γέγονεν ὅτι ἡμῖν μέλλεις

ἐμφανίζειν σεαυτὸν καὶ οὐχὶ τῷ κόσμῳ; **23** ἀπεκρίθη Ἰησοῦς καὶ εἶπεν αὐτῷ· ἐάν τις

ἀγαπᾷ με τὸν λόγον μου τηρήσει, καὶ ὁ πατήρ μου ἀγαπήσει αὐτὸν καὶ πρὸς αὐτὸν

ἐλευσόμεθα καὶ μονὴν παρ᾽ αὐτῷ ποιησόμεθα. **24** ὁ μὴ ἀγαπῶν με τοὺς λόγους μου οὐ

τηρεῖ· καὶ ὁ λόγος ὃν ἀκούετε οὐκ ἔστιν ἐμὸς ἀλλὰ τοῦ πέμψαντός με πατρός.

**John 1:1** Ἐν ἀρχῇ ἦν ὁ λόγος, καὶ ὁ λόγος ἦν πρὸς τὸν θεόν, καὶ θεὸς ἦν ὁ λόγος.

2 οὗτος ἦν ἐν ἀρχῇ πρὸς τὸν θεόν.    3 πάντα δι᾽ αὐτοῦ ἐγένετο, καὶ χωρὶς αὐτοῦ

ἐγένετο οὐδὲ ἕν. ὃ γέγονεν   4 ἐν αὐτῷ ζωὴ ἦν, καὶ ἡ ζωὴ ἦν τὸ φῶς τῶν ἀνθρώπων·

5 καὶ τὸ φῶς ἐν τῇ σκοτίᾳ φαίνει, καὶ ἡ σκοτία αὐτὸ οὐ κατέλαβεν. 6 Ἐγένετο

ἄνθρωπος, ἀπεσταλμένος παρὰ θεοῦ, ὄνομα αὐτῷ Ἰωάννης· 7 οὗτος ἦλθεν εἰς μαρτυρίαν

ἵνα μαρτυρήσῃ περὶ τοῦ φωτός, ἵνα πάντες πιστεύσωσιν δι᾽ αὐτοῦ. 8 οὐκ ἦν ἐκεῖνος τὸ

φῶς, ἀλλ᾽ ἵνα μαρτυρήσῃ περὶ τοῦ φωτός. 9 Ἦν τὸ φῶς τὸ ἀληθινόν, ὃ φωτίζει πάντα

ἄνθρωπον, ἐρχόμενον εἰς τὸν κόσμον. 10 ἐν τῷ κόσμῳ ἦν, καὶ ὁ κόσμος δι᾽ αὐτοῦ

ἐγένετο, καὶ ὁ κόσμος αὐτὸν οὐκ ἔγνω. 11 εἰς τὰ ἴδια ἦλθεν, καὶ οἱ ἴδιοι αὐτὸν οὐ

παρέλαβον. 12 ὅσοι δὲ ἔλαβον αὐτόν, ἔδωκεν αὐτοῖς ἐξουσίαν τέκνα θεοῦ γενέσθαι,

τοῖς πιστεύουσιν εἰς τὸ ὄνομα αὐτοῦ, 13 οἳ οὐκ ἐξ αἱμάτων οὐδὲ ἐκ θελήματος σαρκὸς

οὐδὲ ἐκ θελήματος ἀνδρὸς ἀλλ᾽ ἐκ θεοῦ ἐγεννήθησαν. 14 Καὶ ὁ λόγος σὰρξ ἐγένετο καὶ

ἐσκήνωσεν ἐν ἡμῖν, καὶ ἐθεασάμεθα τὴν δόξαν αὐτοῦ, δόξαν ὡς μονογενοῦς παρὰ

πατρός, πλήρης χάριτος καὶ ἀληθείας. 15 Ἰωάννης μαρτυρεῖ περὶ αὐτοῦ καὶ κέκραγεν λέγων· οὗτος ἦν ὃν εἶπον· ὁ ὀπίσω μου ἐρχόμενος ἔμπροσθέν μου γέγονεν, ὅτι πρῶτός

μου ἦν. **16** ὅτι ἐκ τοῦ πληρώματος αὐτοῦ ἡμεῖς πάντες ἐλάβομεν καὶ χάριν ἀντὶ

χάριτος· **17** ὅτι ὁ νόμος διὰ Μωϋσέως ἐδόθη, ἡ χάρις καὶ ἡ ἀλήθεια διὰ Ἰησοῦ

Χριστοῦ ἐγένετο. **18** Θεὸν οὐδεὶς ἑώρακεν πώποτε· μονογενὴς θεὸς ὁ ὢν εἰς τὸν

κόλπον τοῦ πατρὸς ἐκεῖνος ἐξηγήσατο.


**Colossians 1:13** ὃς ἐρρύσατο ἡμᾶς ἐκ τῆς ἐξουσίας τοῦ σκότους καὶ μετέστησεν εἰς

τὴν βασιλείαν τοῦ υἱοῦ τῆς ἀγάπης αὐτοῦ, **14** ἐν ᾧ ἔχομεν τὴν ἀπολύτρωσιν, τὴν

ἄφεσιν τῶν ἁμαρτιῶν· **15** ὅς ἐστιν εἰκὼν τοῦ θεοῦ τοῦ ἀοράτου, πρωτότοκος πάσης

κτίσεως, **16** ὅτι ἐν αὐτῷ ἐκτίσθη τὰ πάντα ἐν τοῖς οὐρανοῖς καὶ ἐπὶ τῆς γῆς, τὰ ὁρατὰ

καὶ τὰ ἀόρατα, εἴτε θρόνοι εἴτε κυριότητες εἴτε ἀρχαὶ εἴτε ἐξουσίαι· τὰ πάντα δι᾽

αὐτοῦ καὶ εἰς αὐτὸν ἔκτισται· **17** καὶ αὐτός ἐστιν πρὸ πάντων καὶ τὰ πάντα ἐν αὐτῷ

συνέστηκεν, **18** καὶ αὐτός ἐστιν ἡ κεφαλὴ τοῦ σώματος τῆς ἐκκλησίας· ὅς ἐστιν ἀρχή,

πρωτότοκος ἐκ τῶν νεκρῶν, ἵνα γένηται ἐν πᾶσιν αὐτὸς πρωτεύων, **19** ὅτι ἐν αὐτῷ

εὐδόκησεν πᾶν τὸ πλήρωμα κατοικῆσαι **20** καὶ δι᾽ αὐτοῦ ἀποκαταλλάξαι τὰ πάντα εἰς αὐτόν, εἰρηνοποιήσας διὰ τοῦ αἵματος τοῦ σταυροῦ αὐτοῦ, [δι᾽ αὐτοῦ] εἴτε τὰ ἐπὶ τῆς

γῆς εἴτε τὰ ἐν τοῖς οὐρανοῖς. 21 Καὶ ὑμᾶς ποτε ὄντας ἀπηλλοτριωμένους καὶ ἐχθροὺς

τῇ διανοίᾳ ἐν τοῖς ἔργοις τοῖς πονηροῖς,     22 νυνὶ δὲ ἀποκατήλλαξεν ἐν τῷ σώματι

τῆς σαρκὸς αὐτοῦ διὰ τοῦ θανάτου παραστῆσαι ὑμᾶς ἁγίους καὶ ἀμώμους καὶ

ἀνεγκλήτους κατενώπιον αὐτοῦ, 23 εἴ γε ἐπιμένετε τῇ πίστει τεθεμελιωμένοι καὶ

ἑδραῖοι καὶ μὴ μετακινούμενοι ἀπὸ τῆς ἐλπίδος τοῦ εὐαγγελίου οὗ ἠκούσατε, τοῦ

κηρυχθέντος ἐν πάσῃ κτίσει τῇ ὑπὸ τὸν οὐρανόν, οὗ ἐγενόμην ἐγὼ Παῦλος διάκονος.

# QUESTIONS FOR HEART AND MIND

## CHRIST/SON

## JOHN 1:1-18

1. Identify five attributes of Christ in this passage.

2. What works are ascribed to Christ?

3. What is the significance of the preposition in, "All things came to pass *through* him" (1:3)?

4. What proof is there here for the deity and the humanity of Christ?

5. Give three significant truths about Christ as derived from verse 18.

6. How does one refute the use of John 1:1 ("*a* god") by Jehovah's Witnesses?

# QUESTIONS FOR HEART AND MIND

## CHRIST/SON

### COLOSSIANS 1:13-23

1. List five statements about the person of Christ from verses 15-20. How is his deity implicit?

2. What is the heresy known as Arianism, and how did it use this passage?

   What argues against it?

3. What is Christ's relationship to the creation according to verses 16-17?

4. How do verses 15-20 relate to verses 13-14?

5. What does "all the fullness" mean (v. 19)?

6. What heresy is based upon the "all" of verse 20?

7. What is the relationship of verses 21-23 to verses 15-20?

LESSON THREE

# CLASS DISCUSSION QUESTIONS

## NOMINATIVE, VOCATIVE, GENITIVE, ABLATIVE, DATIVE, LOCATIVE CASES

### CHRIST/SON

### JOHN 1:1-18

1.      How should the last clause of John 1:1 be translated?


        How do we determine what is the subject and what is the predicate nominative?


2.      What is the referrent of θεόν in the second clause?


        What is the referrent of θεὸς in third clause?


        Why could John not use the articular form in the third clause?


3.      Are the Jehovah Witnesses correct when they translate the third clause, "and the word was a god"?

        Why or why not?


4.      What is the significance of the anarthrous θεὸς (cf. the articular form in the second clause)?

## CLASS DISCUSSION QUESTIONS

### NOMINATIVE, VOCATIVE, GENITIVE, ABLATIVE, DATIVE, LOCATIVE CASES

### CHRIST/SON

### COLOSSIANS 1:13-23

1.      What are the possible functions for τοῦ θεοῦ (1:15) and the implications?

2.      What are the possible functions for κτίσεως (1:15) and the implications?

        Which views lead to heresy?

3.      Note the three prepositions used of Christ's role in creation (v. 16) and answer the following questions:

        What are the possible meanings of each?

        What are the theological implications of each?

        What prepositions are not used but are available?

        What do the parallel passages (John 1:3; Heb. 1:2) contribute?

# CASES

**ABLATIVE (Separation)**

| | | | | |
|---|---|---|---|---|
| 1. Separation | Separation | Ac.27:43; Eph.2:12 | 21 | 107 |
| 2. Source | (Source) from | Ac.1:4; Rom.15:4 | 23 | 109 |
| 3. Agency | Personal | Mt.25:34; Rom.1:7 | 24 | 126 |
| 4. Means | Impersonal | 1 Cor.2:13; Rom.4:11 | 26 | 125 |
| 5. Comparison | "than" | Mt.3:11; 1 Jn.3:20 | 27 | 110 |
| 6. Direct Object | Verbs of ceasing, missing, lacking, despairing, comparing | Ac.17:25 | -- | 131 |
| 7. Apposition | Identity ("namely") | | -- | 94 |
| 8. With Prepositions | αντι, απο, δια, εκ, κατα, παρα, περι, προ, υπο | | 60-62 | 136 |

**DATIVE (Interest)**

| | | | | |
|---|---|---|---|---|
| 1. Indirect Object | "To, For whom" | Mt.13:13; 18:26 | 32 | 140 |
| 2. Advantage, Disadvan. (ethical) | "For" "Against" | 2 Cor.2:1; Rev.21:2 Mt.23:31 | 33 | 142 |
| 3. Possession | Ownership | Jn.1:6; Lk.1:7 | 35 | 149 |
| 4. Reference (respect) | "With reference to" | Rom.8:12; 6:2 | 36 | 144 |
| 5. Direct Object | Verbs of serving, pleasing, helping, believing, worshiping, etc. | Rom.7:25; Jn.3:36 | 37 | 171 |
| 6. Apposition | Identity ("namely") | | -- | 152 |
| 7. With Prepositions | εν, επι | | 60-62 | 175 |

**LOCATIVE (Position)**

| | | | | |
|---|---|---|---|---|
| 1. Place | Spatial (literal) | Mk.3:34; Ac.5:31 | 38 | 153 |
| 2. Time | Point of Time | Lk.24:1; Mt.20:19 | 39 | 155 |
| 3. Sphere | Logical; Figurative | 1 Cor.14:20; Mt.5:3 | 40 | 153 |
| 4. Apposition | Identity ("namely") | | -- | 152 |
| 5. With Prepositions | εν, επι, παρα, προς | | 60-62 | 175 |

# ASSIGNMENT

## IDENTIFY SYNTACTICAL FORMS/FUNCTIONS:  THE CASES

## NOMINATIVE, VOCATIVE, GENITIVE, ABLATIVE, DATIVE, LOCATIVE

### JOHN 1:1-18

Identify the case and its function

1. λόγος  (v. 1)

2. πάντα  (v. 3)

3. φῶς  (v. 4)

4. ἀνθρώπων

5. ὄνομα  (v. 6)

6. Ἰωάννης

7. φωτός  (v. 7)

8. φῶς  (v. 8)

9. αὐτοῦ  (v. 10)

10. ἴδιοι  (v. 11)

11. ὅσοι  (v. 12)

12. θεοῦ

13. αὐτου

14. σαρκὸς  (v. 13)

15. σὰρξ  (v. 14)

16. χάριτος

17. μου  (v. 15)

18. μου  (3d usage)

19. θεὸς  (v. 18)

20. πατρὸς

# ASSIGNMENT

## IDENTIFY SYNTACTICAL FORMS/FUNCTIONS:  CASES

## NOMINATIVE, VOCATIVE, GENITIVE, ABLATIVE, DATIVE, LOCATIVE

## COLOSSIANS 1:13-23

Identify the case and its function

1. σκότους  (v. 13)

2. ἀγάπης

3. αὐτου

4. ᾧ  (v. 14)

5. ἁμαρτιῶν

6. εἰκὼν (v. 15)

7. θεοῦ

8. πρωτότοκος

9. κτίσεως

10. πάντα  (v. 16)

11. γῆς

12. ὁρατὰ

13. θρόνοι

14. αὐτοῦ

15. πάντων  (v. 17)

16. κεφαλὴ  (v. 18)

17. σώματος

18. ἐκκλησίας

19. πρωτότοκος

20. πρωτεύων

21. πλήρωμα  (v. 19)

22. σταυροῦ  (v. 20)

23. σαρκὸς  (v. 22)

24. εὐαγγελίου  (v. 23)

25. Παῦλος

26. διάκονος

# LESSON FOUR:
## SYMBOLISM ABOUT CHRIST/HOLY SPIRIT

### Angel

The word "angel" means "messenger," and angels most often appear in the context of a message from God. Examples are the Annunciation to Mary, the appearance to shepherds at Christmas, the announcement of the Resurrection, and many others. Angels may also represent the watchfulness or presence of God.

### Scepter

The scepter is a symbol of authority. Together with the crown, it is a symbol of Christ's triumphant reign over all creation.

### Shell

The shell (usually a scallop or cockle shell) with three water drops is a symbol of baptism generally, and especially of the baptism of Christ. The three droplets remind us of the Trinity - Father, Son and Holy Spirit - into which Christians are baptized. The shell alone may also be used as a symbol for pilgrimage, and may be used as an emblem for saints known for their travels (such as St. James) or whose shrines have become destinations for pilgrims.

### Dove

The dove is a symbol of the Holy Spirit. It is taken from the story of Jesus' baptism, where the Spirit descended on him in the form of a dove. The three-rayed nimbus around its head identifies the Spirit as a member of the Trinity. A dove shown without the nimbus is a symbol of peace.

# LESSON FOUR

## CHRIST/HOLY SPIRIT

**John 14:25** Ταῦτα λελάληκα ὑμῖν παρ᾽ ὑμῖν μένων· **26** ὁ δὲ παράκλητος, τὸ πνεῦμα

τὸ ἅγιον, ὃ πέμψει ὁ πατὴρ ἐν τῷ ὀνόματί μου, ἐκεῖνος ὑμᾶς διδάξει πάντα καὶ

ὑπομνήσει ὑμᾶς πάντα ἃ εἶπον ὑμῖν [ἐγώ]. **27** Εἰρήνην ἀφίημι ὑμῖν, εἰρήνην τὴν ἐμὴν

δίδωμι ὑμῖν· οὐ καθὼς ὁ κόσμος δίδωσιν ἐγὼ δίδωμι ὑμῖν. μὴ ταρασσέσθω ὑμῶν ἡ

καρδία μηδὲ δειλιάτω. **28** ἠκούσατε ὅτι ἐγὼ εἶπον ὑμῖν· ὑπάγω καὶ ἔρχομαι πρὸς ὑμᾶς.

εἰ ἠγαπᾶτέ με ἐχάρητε ἂν ὅτι πορεύομαι πρὸς τὸν πατέρα, ὅτι ὁ πατὴρ μείζων μού

ἐστιν. **29** καὶ νῦν εἴρηκα ὑμῖν πρὶν γενέσθαι, ἵνα ὅταν γένηται πιστεύσητε.


**Hebrews 1:1** Πολυμερῶς καὶ πολυτρόπως πάλαι ὁ θεὸς λαλήσας τοῖς πατράσιν ἐν τοῖς

προφήταις **2** ἐπ᾽ ἐσχάτου τῶν ἡμερῶν τούτων ἐλάλησεν ἡμῖν ἐν υἱῷ, ὃν ἔθηκεν

κληρονόμον πάντων, δι᾽ οὗ καὶ ἐποίησεν τοὺς αἰῶνας· **3** ὃς ὢν ἀπαύγασμα τῆς δόξης

καὶ χαρακτὴρ τῆς ὑποστάσεως αὐτοῦ, φέρων τε τὰ πάντα τῷ ῥήματι τῆς δυνάμεως

αὐτοῦ, καθαρισμὸν τῶν ἁμαρτιῶν ποιησάμενος ἐκάθισεν ἐν δεξιᾷ τῆς μεγαλωσύνης ἐν ὑψηλοῖς, **4** τοσούτῳ κρείττων γενόμενος τῶν ἀγγέλων ὅσῳ διαφορώτερον παρ' αὐτοὺς

κεκληρονόμηκεν ὄνομα. **5** Τίνι γὰρ εἶπέν ποτε τῶν ἀγγέλων· υἱός μου εἶ σύ, ἐγὼ

σήμερον γεγέννηκά σε; καὶ πάλιν· ἐγὼ ἔσομαι αὐτῷ εἰς πατέρα, καὶ αὐτὸς ἔσται μοι εἰς

υἱόν; **6** ὅταν δὲ πάλιν εἰσαγάγῃ τὸν πρωτότοκον εἰς τὴν οἰκουμένην, λέγει· καὶ

προσκυνησάτωσαν αὐτῷ πάντες ἄγγελοι θεοῦ. **7** καὶ πρὸς μὲν τοὺς ἀγγέλους λέγει· ὁ

ποιῶν τοὺς ἀγγέλους αὐτοῦ πνεύματα καὶ τοὺς λειτουργοὺς αὐτοῦ πυρὸς φλόγα, **8** πρὸς

δὲ τὸν υἱόν· ὁ θρόνος σου ὁ θεὸς εἰς τὸν αἰῶνα τοῦ αἰῶνος, καὶ ἡ ῥάβδος τῆς

εὐθύτητος ῥάβδος τῆς βασιλείας σου. **9** ἠγάπησας δικαιοσύνην καὶ ἐμίσησας ἀνομίαν·

διὰ τοῦτο ἔχρισέν σε ὁ θεὸς ὁ θεός σου ἔλαιον ἀγαλλιάσεως παρὰ τοὺς μετόχους σου.

**10** καί· σὺ κατ' ἀρχάς, κύριε, τὴν γῆν ἐθεμελίωσας, καὶ ἔργα τῶν χειρῶν σού εἰσιν οἱ

οὐρανοί· **11** αὐτοὶ ἀπολοῦνται, σὺ δὲ διαμένεις, καὶ πάντες ὡς ἱμάτιον

παλαιωθήσονται, **12** καὶ ὡσεὶ περιβόλαιον ἑλίξεις αὐτούς, ὡς ἱμάτιον καὶ

ἀλλαγήσονται· σὺ δὲ ὁ αὐτὸς εἶ καὶ τὰ ἔτη σου οὐκ ἐκλείψουσιν. **13** πρὸς τίνα δὲ τῶν

ἀγγέλων εἴρηκέν ποτε· κάθου ἐκ δεξιῶν μου, ἕως ἂν θῶ τοὺς ἐχθρούς σου ὑποπόδιον τῶν ποδῶν σου; **14** οὐχὶ πάντες εἰσὶν λειτουργικὰ πνεύματα εἰς διακονίαν

ἀποστελλόμενα διὰ τοὺς μέλλοντας κληρονομεῖν σωτηρίαν;

**Acts 2:1** Καὶ ἐν τῷ συμπληροῦσθαι τὴν ἡμέραν τῆς πεντηκοστῆς ἦσαν πάντες ὁμοῦ ἐπὶ

τὸ αὐτό. **2** καὶ ἐγένετο ἄφνω ἐκ τοῦ οὐρανοῦ ἦχος ὥσπερ φερομένης πνοῆς βιαίας καὶ

ἐπλήρωσεν ὅλον τὸν οἶκον οὗ ἦσαν καθήμενοι **3** καὶ ὤφθησαν αὐτοῖς διαμεριζόμεναι

γλῶσσαι ὡσεὶ πυρὸς καὶ ἐκάθισεν ἐφ᾽ ἕνα ἕκαστον αὐτῶν, **4** καὶ ἐπλήσθησαν πάντες

πνεύματος ἁγίου καὶ ἤρξαντο λαλεῖν ἑτέραις γλώσσαις καθὼς τὸ πνεῦμα ἐδίδου

ἀποφθέγγεσθαι αὐτοῖς.

\ \ \ \ \ \

**Acts 2:14** Σταθεὶς δὲ ὁ Πέτρος σὺν τοῖς ἕνδεκα ἐπῆρεν τὴν φωνὴν αὐτοῦ καὶ

ἀπεφθέγξατο αὐτοῖς· ἄνδρες Ἰουδαῖοι καὶ οἱ κατοικοῦντες Ἰερουσαλὴμ πάντες, τοῦτο

ὑμῖν γνωστὸν ἔστω καὶ ἐνωτίσασθε τὰ ῥήματά μου. **15** οὐ γὰρ ὡς ὑμεῖς ὑπολαμβάνετε

οὗτοι μεθύουσιν, ἔστιν γὰρ ὥρα τρίτη τῆς ἡμέρας, **16** ἀλλὰ τοῦτό ἐστιν τὸ εἰρημένον

διὰ τοῦ προφήτου Ἰωήλ· **17** καὶ ἔσται ἐν ταῖς ἐσχάταις ἡμέραις, λέγει ὁ θεός, ἐκχεῶ

ἀπὸ τοῦ πνεύματός μου ἐπὶ πᾶσαν σάρκα, καὶ προφητεύσουσιν οἱ υἱοὶ ὑμῶν καὶ αἱ θυγατέρες ὑμῶν καὶ οἱ νεανίσκοι ὑμῶν ὁράσεις ὄψονται καὶ οἱ πρεσβύτεροι ὑμῶν

ἐνυπνίοις ἐνυπνιασθήσονται· 18 καί γε ἐπὶ τοὺς δούλους μου καὶ ἐπὶ τὰς δούλας μου

ἐν ταῖς ἡμέραις ἐκείναις ἐκχεῶ ἀπὸ τοῦ πνεύματός μου, καὶ προφητεύσουσιν. 19 καὶ

δώσω τέρατα ἐν τῷ οὐρανῷ ἄνω καὶ σημεῖα ἐπὶ τῆς γῆς κάτω, αἷμα καὶ πῦρ καὶ

ἀτμίδα καπνοῦ. 20 ὁ ἥλιος μεταστραφήσεται εἰς σκότος καὶ ἡ σελήνη εἰς αἷμα, πρὶν

ἐλθεῖν ἡμέραν κυρίου τὴν μεγάλην καὶ ἐπιφανῆ. 21 καὶ ἔσται πᾶς ὃς ἂν ἐπικαλέσηται

τὸ ὄνομα κυρίου σωθήσεται.

# QUESTIONS FOR HEART AND MIND

## CHRIST

### HEBREWS 1:1-14

1. Give five attributes or works of Christ derived from 1:1-4. Give five from 1:5-13.

2. What phrase regarding Christ's role in creation ties the passage to John 1 and Col. 1?

3. What word shows the unity of God's revelation (vv. 1-2) and how does the author support this (vv. 5-13)?

4. What is significant about the change in tense of the participles in verse 3?

5. What is the significance of "right hand of God" and from where does it derive (cf. 1:13-14)?

6. What does the passage contribute to the idea of prayer?

# QUESTIONS FOR HEART AND MIND

## HOLY SPIRIT

### ACTS 2:1-4, 14-21

1. How do the events of this reading relate to Acts 1 and to John 14:25-29?

2. When Peter addresses the crowd, were women also present (see vv. 17-18, 21)?

   What does this tell us about the meaning of "men, Jews, and all those who dwell in Jerusalem"?

3. Was the prophecy of Joel 2:28-32 fulfilled? What is Peter's actual terminology (v. 16)?

   What are the implications for eschatology and ecclesiology if it was fulfilled?

4. What implications do the words of verses 19-20 have for hermeneutics?

   What implications do the additions made by Peter to Joel in verses 17-18 have for hermeneutics?

## CLASS DISCUSSION QUESTIONS

### NOMINATIVE, VOCATIVE, GENITIVE, ABLATIVE
### DATIVE, LOCATIVE, INSTRUMENTAL, ACCUSATIVE CASES

### CHRIST

### HEBREWS 1:1-14

1.  What is the function of the accusative σήμερον (1:5)?

    What are the theological implications of "today," i.e., when is "today"?

    What did it mean to the psalmist (Ps. 2:7)?

    What did it mean to Paul (Acts 13:13)?

2.  What use of the double accusative occurs in verse 2?  Cite the words.

    In verse 7 (twice)?  Cite the words.

    In verse 13?  Again, cite the words.

3.  What use of the instrumental case is ῥήματι (v. 3)?

    What is the use of the instrumental in the words τοσούτῳ . . . ὅσῳ  (v. 4)?

4.  What use of the accusative is ἔλαιον  (v. 9)?  Is it another instance of a double accusative?

## CLASS DISCUSSION QUESTIONS

### NOMINATIVE, VOCATIVE, GENITIVE, ABLATIVE
### DATIVE, LOCATIVE, INSTRUMENTAL, ACCUSATIVE CASES

### HOLY SPIRIT

### ACTS 2:1-4, 14-21

1. In verses 2 and 4, compare the objects of the two verbs ἐπλήρωσεν and ἐπλήσθησαν. What cases are involved and why is there a difference?

2. What two different cases are represented by ἡμέρας (v. 15) and ἡμέραις (v. 17) and used as temporal indicators?

   What different emphases do the cases make?

3. What are the possibilities for the function of the genitive κυρίου in verse 21?

   What are the resultant meanings?   Which seems best?

# CASES

## INSTRUMENTAL (Means)

| | | | | |
|---|---|---|---|---|
| 1. Means | Impersonal | Mk.5:4; Lk.6:1 | 42 | 162 |
| 2. Cause | "Because" | Rom.11:30; Lk.15:17 | 43 | 167 |
| | Means and Reason | | | |
| | External-Internal | | | |
| 3. Manner | How | 1 Cor.10:30; 11:5; Ac.11:23 | 44 | 161 |
| 4. Measure | Interval of Time, Degree | Lk.8:27; Rom.16:25 | 45 | 166 |
| 5. Association (comit. dat.) | Second Person in Accompany; Direct Obj. | Rom.11:2; 1 Cor.4:8 | 47 | 159 |
| 6. Agency | Personal Means | Lk.23:15; Gal.5:18 | 48 | 163 |
| 7. Apposition | Identity ("namely") | | -- | 152 |
| 8. With Prepositions | εν, επι, παρα, συν | | 60-62 | 175 |

## ACCUSATIVE (Limitation)

| | | | | |
|---|---|---|---|---|
| 1. Direct Object | Receives Action | Mt.4:21; Jn.8:46 | 49 | 179 |
| 2. Cognate | Same Root, Idea | Mk.4:41; 1 Pet.5:2 | 50 | 189 |
| 3. Double | | | | |
|   a. Personal & Impersonal | "teach, ask, clothe" | Heb.5:12; Jn.14:26 | -- | 181 |
|   b. Direct & Obj. Complem. | "call, elect, have" | Ac.13:5; Jn.15:15 | 51 | 182 |
| 4. Adverbial | Adverb, Modifies Verb | | | |
|   a. Measure | Extent of Time/Space | Mt.20:6; Jn.6:19 | 52 | 201 |
|   b. Manner | "How", "With" | Lk.16:19; Mt.10:8 | 55 | 200 |
|   c. Reference, Respect | "With reference to" | Jn.6:10; Rom.10:5 | 55 | 203 |
| 5. Sub. of Infinitive | (cf. Acc.of Gen.Ref.) | Lk.18:16; 1 Co.10:13; He.5:12 | 55-6 | 192 |
| 6. With Oaths | "By____" (swearing) | Ac.19:13; 1 Thes. 5:27 | 57 | 204 |
| 7. Absolute | Independent (rare) | Ac.26:3; Eph.1:18 | 58 | 198 |
| 8. Apposition | Identity ("namely") | | -- | 198 |
| 9. With Prepositions | ανα, δια, εις, επι, κατα, μετα, παρα, περι, προς, υπερ, υπο | | 60-62 | 205 |

# ASSIGNMENT

## IDENTIFY SYNTACTICAL FORMS/FUNCTIONS: CASES

### NOMINATIVE, VOCATIVE, GENITIVE, ABLATIVE
### DATIVE, LOCATIVE, INSTRUMENTAL, ACCUSATIVE

### HEBREWS 1:1-14

Identify the case and its function

1. πατράσιν (v. 1)

2. προφήταις

3. ἡμερῶν (v. 2)

4. ἡμῖν

5. πάντων

6. οὗ

7. ἀπαύγασμα (v. 3)

8. δόξης

9. ὑποστάσεως

10. ῥήματι

11. δυνάμεως

12. ἁμαρτιῶν

13. δεξιᾷ

14. μεγαλωσύνης

15. κρείττων (v. 4)

16. ἀγγέλων

17. ὅσῳ

18. Τίνι (v. 5)

19. ἀγγέλων

20. υἱός

21. αὐτῷ

22. αὐτῷ (v. 6)

23. θεὸς (v. 8)

24. αἰῶνος

25. εὐθύτητος

26. θεός (v. 9)

27. ἀγαλλιάσεως

28. χειρῶν (v. 10)

29. ὑποπόδιον (v. 13)

30. ποδῶν

# ASSIGNMENT

## IDENTIFY SYNTACTICAL FORMS/FUNCTIONS: CASES

### NOMINATIVE, VOCATIVE, GENITIVE, ABLATIVE
### DATIVE, LOCATIVE, INSTRUMENTAL, ACCUSATIVE

### ACTS 2:1-4, 14-21

Identify the case and its function

1. ἡμέραν (v. 1)

2. πεντηκοστῆς

3. πνοῆς (v. 2)

4. οἶκον

5. αὐτοῖς (v. 3)

6. πυρός

7. αὐτῶν

8. πνεύματος (v. 4)

9. γλώσσαις

10. πνεῦμα

11. Πέτρος (v. 14)

12. φωνὴν

13. αὐτοῖς

14. Ἄνδρες

15. Ἰουδαῖοι

16. τοῦτο

17. ὥρα (v. 15)

18. ἡμέρας

19. Ἰωήλ (v. 16)

20. ὁράσεις (v. 17)

21. ἐνυπνίοις

22. αἷμα (v. 19)

23. πῦρ

24. ἡμέραν (v. 20)

25. κυρίου

26. κυρίου (v. 21)

# CASE STUDY ON CHRISTOLOGY

## THE COUNCIL OF NICEA (A.D. 325)

1. Issues:

2. Persons and their theological positions:

3. Resolutions:

4. Resources of grace:

5. Unresolved issues:

# LESSON FIVE:
# SYMBOLISM ABOUT SATAN/SPIRITUAL WARFARE

## Serpent

A serpent coiled around a fruiting tree is a symbol taken from the Genesis account of the Fall. Though not named in Genesis, the serpent is understood to be Satan. The tree is the Tree of the Knowledge of Good and Evil, one of two trees from which Adam and Eve were not to eat (the other was the Tree of Life). The fruit, usually represented by an apple, is the tree's "forbidden fruit."

## *Agnus Dei*

The *Agnus Dei* (Latin for "Lamb of God") may appear in several postures. Standing with a banner, it represents the risen Christ who triumphs over death. Standing with a cross and bleeding from a gash in its side, it represents the suffering and death of our Lord. Seated on a book with seven seals, it represents the final judgment when Christ returns in glory. This symbol is rich in significance. John the Baptist proclaimed Jesus to be the Lamb of God who takes away the sin of the world. In the Revelation, Jesus is portrayed as a lamb. Even in the Old Testament, God's provision of a ram as a substitute sacrifice for Isaac is an important type of Christ.

# LESSON FIVE

## SATAN/SPIRITUAL WARFARE

**John 14:30** οὐκέτι πολλὰ λαλήσω μεθ᾽ ὑμῶν, ἔρχεται γὰρ ὁ τοῦ κόσμου ἄρχων· καὶ ἐν

ἐμοὶ οὐκ ἔχει οὐδέν, **31** ἀλλ᾽ ἵνα γνῷ ὁ κόσμος ὅτι ἀγαπῶ τὸν πατέρα, καὶ καθὼς

ἐνετείλατό μοι ὁ πατήρ, οὕτως ποιῶ. ἐγείρεσθε, ἄγωμεν ἐντεῦθεν.


**Matthew 4:1** Τότε ὁ Ἰησοῦς ἀνήχθη εἰς τὴν ἔρημον ὑπὸ τοῦ πνεύματος πειρασθῆναι

ὑπὸ τοῦ διαβόλου. **2** καὶ νηστεύσας ἡμέρας τεσσεράκοντα καὶ νύκτας τεσσεράκοντα,

ὕστερον ἐπείνασεν. **3** καὶ προσελθὼν ὁ πειράζων εἶπεν αὐτῷ· εἰ υἱὸς εἶ τοῦ θεοῦ, εἰπὲ

ἵνα οἱ λίθοι οὗτοι ἄρτοι γένωνται. **4** ὁ δὲ ἀποκριθεὶς εἶπεν· γέγραπται· οὐκ ἐπ᾽ ἄρτῳ

μόνῳ ζήσεται ὁ ἄνθρωπος, ἀλλ᾽ ἐπὶ παντὶ ῥήματι ἐκπορευομένῳ διὰ στόματος θεοῦ. **5**

Τότε παραλαμβάνει αὐτὸν ὁ διάβολος εἰς τὴν ἁγίαν πόλιν καὶ ἔστησεν αὐτὸν ἐπὶ τὸ

πτερύγιον τοῦ ἱεροῦ **6** καὶ λέγει αὐτῷ· εἰ υἱὸς εἶ τοῦ θεοῦ, βάλε σεαυτὸν κάτω·

γέγραπται γὰρ ὅτι τοῖς ἀγγέλοις αὐτοῦ ἐντελεῖται περὶ σοῦ καὶ ἐπὶ χειρῶν ἀροῦσίν

σε, μήποτε προσκόψῃς πρὸς λίθον τὸν πόδα σου. **7** ἔφη αὐτῷ ὁ Ἰησοῦς· πάλιν γέγραπται· οὐκ ἐκπειράσεις κύριον τὸν θεόν σου. **8** Πάλιν παραλαμβάνει αὐτὸν ὁ

διάβολος εἰς ὄρος ὑψηλὸν λίαν καὶ δείκνυσιν αὐτῷ πάσας τὰς βασιλείας τοῦ κόσμου

καὶ τὴν δόξαν αὐτῶν **9** καὶ εἶπεν αὐτῷ· ταῦτά σοι πάντα δώσω, ἐὰν πεσὼν

προσκυνήσῃς μοι. **10** τότε λέγει αὐτῷ ὁ Ἰησοῦς· ὕπαγε, σατανᾶ· γέγραπται γάρ· κύριον

τὸν θεόν σου προσκυνήσεις καὶ αὐτῷ μόνῳ λατρεύσεις. **11** Τότε ἀφίησιν αὐτὸν ὁ

διάβολος, καὶ ἰδοὺ ἄγγελοι προσῆλθον καὶ διηκόνουν αὐτῷ.

**Ephesians 6:10** Τοῦ λοιποῦ, ἐνδυναμοῦσθε ἐν κυρίῳ καὶ ἐν τῷ κράτει τῆς ἰσχύος

αὐτοῦ. **11** ἐνδύσασθε τὴν πανοπλίαν τοῦ θεοῦ πρὸς τὸ δύνασθαι ὑμᾶς στῆναι πρὸς τὰς

μεθοδείας τοῦ διαβόλου· **12** ὅτι οὐκ ἔστιν ἡμῖν ἡ πάλη πρὸς αἷμα καὶ σάρκα ἀλλὰ πρὸς

τὰς ἀρχάς, πρὸς τὰς ἐξουσίας, πρὸς τοὺς κοσμοκράτορας τοῦ σκότους τούτου, πρὸς τὰ

πνευματικὰ τῆς πονηρίας ἐν τοῖς ἐπουρανίοις. **13** διὰ τοῦτο ἀναλάβετε τὴν πανοπλίαν

τοῦ θεοῦ, ἵνα δυνηθῆτε ἀντιστῆναι ἐν τῇ ἡμέρᾳ τῇ πονηρᾷ καὶ ἅπαντα κατεργασάμενοι

στῆναι. **14** στῆτε οὖν περιζωσάμενοι τὴν ὀσφὺν ὑμῶν ἐν ἀληθείᾳ καὶ ἐνδυσάμενοι τὸν

θώρακα τῆς δικαιοσύνης **15** καὶ ὑποδησάμενοι τοὺς πόδας ἐν ἑτοιμασίᾳ τοῦ εὐαγγελίου τῆς εἰρήνης, **16** ἐν πᾶσιν ἀναλαβόντες τὸν θυρεὸν τῆς πίστεως, ἐν ᾧ δυνήσεσθε πάντα

τὰ βέλη τοῦ πονηροῦ [τὰ] πεπυρωμένα σβέσαι· **17** καὶ τὴν περικεφαλαίαν τοῦ σωτηρίου

δέξασθε καὶ τὴν μάχαιραν τοῦ πνεύματος, ὅ ἐστιν ῥῆμα θεοῦ. **18** Διὰ πάσης προσευχῆς

καὶ δεήσεως προσευχόμενοι ἐν παντὶ καιρῷ ἐν πνεύματι, καὶ εἰς αὐτὸ ἀγρυπνοῦντες ἐν

πάσῃ προσκαρτερήσει καὶ δεήσει περὶ πάντων τῶν ἁγίων **19** καὶ ὑπὲρ ἐμοῦ, ἵνα μοι

δοθῇ λόγος ἐν ἀνοίξει τοῦ στόματός μου, ἐν παρρησίᾳ γνωρίσαι τὸ μυστήριον τοῦ

εὐαγγελίου, **20** ὑπὲρ οὗ πρεσβεύω ἐν ἁλύσει, ἵνα ἐν αὐτῷ παρρησιάσωμαι ὡς δεῖ με

λαλῆσαι.

# QUESTIONS FOR HEART AND MIND

## SATAN/SPIRITUAL WARFARE

### MATTHEW 4:1-11

1. What titles are used for Satan in this passage?

2. What is the significance of these titles for us today?

3. How did Christ answer Satan?

   What sections of the OT did he appeal to?     Why?

4. What three things might we learn about Satan in this passage?

5. Give three things we learn about temptation and angels.

6. What would have been the consequences if Jesus had yielded on any one of these tests?

7. If we were offered the things of verses 8-9, how would we respond?  Why?

8. Of what significance is Jesus' addition of "alone" to the quotation (v. 10)?

# QUESTIONS FOR HEART AND MIND

## SATAN/SPIRITUAL WARFARE

### EPHESIANS 6:10-20

1. What titles or descriptions are used of Satan and fallen angels here?



    How do these relate to the title used in John 14:30?



2. What is the significance of so many titles?



3. How is the Holy Spirit prominent and why?



4. How is the armor related to protection from Satanic forces?



5. Comparing Matthew 4:1-11 with this passage, what observation can be made regarding prepositions?



6. How do these two passages impact one's worldview regarding what constitutes reality?

# CLASS DISCUSSION QUESTIONS

## PREPOSITIONS

## SATAN/SPIRITUAL WARFARE

## MATTHEW 4:1-11

1.    Note the two uses of ὑπò (in 4:1) and answer the following questions:

What does the preposition mean (give possibilities)?

Are the two uses the same?  Why or why not?

2.    What are the theological implications of each use?  What do we learn about Satan?

3.    How does this usage relate to James 1:13?

# CLASS DISCUSSION QUESTIONS

## PREPOSITIONS

## SATAN/SPIRITUAL WARFARE

## EPHESIANS 6:10-20

1.     Note the use of prepositions in this passage as compared to Matthew 4:1-11. What should we make of this?

2.     What are the possibilities for ἐν in verse 14?

3.     What are the possibilities for ἐν πνεύματι (v. 18)?

4.     What are the possibilities for the second ἐν in verse 20?

# PREPOSITIONS

## I. DEFINITIONS AND DISTINCTIVES

A.  A preposition is an adverb specialized to define, to clarify, a case usage.

B.  A preposition is a word joined to, and usually placed before, a noun or pronoun to show the relation of a noun to something else in the sentence.

C.  The resulting preposition-noun phrase is equivalent to an adjective or an adverb.

D.  Proper prepositions may be compounded with verbs, not improper prepositions.

E.  Meaning is determined by the case idea, meaning of the preposition, and context.

## II. ADVERBIAL PREPOSITIONS=IMPROPER PREPOSITIONS (42)

--All are used with the genitive or ablative case except αμα (instru.) and εγγυς (often also with the dative).

A.  Improper Prepositions Are Used Only With Cases (cannot be compounded with verbs).

| | |
|---|---|
| 1. ανευ | 4. μεχρι |
| 2. ενεκα, ενεκεν | 5. αχρι |
| 3. εως | |

B.  Prepositional Adverbs May Be Used Without Cases.

| | | | |
|---|---|---|---|
| 1. αμα | 5. εναντιον | 9. κυκλοθεν | 13. οψε |
| 2. εγγυς | 6. εντος | 10. λαθρα | 14. περαν |
| 3. εσω | 7. ενωπιον | 11. μεταξυ | 15. πλην |
| 4. εκτος | 8. εξω | 12. οπισθεν | 16. χαριν |
| | | | 17. χωρις |

C.  Proper Prepositions Are Combined With Adverbs.

| | |
|---|---|
| 1. εναντι | 3. επανω |
| 2. εμπροσθεν | 4. υποκατω |

D. Biblical Circumlocutions By Means Of Nouns With The Genitive

1. προσωπον (w. απο)        4. ονομα (εις το ονομα)
2. χειρ (w. δια)            5. μεσον (ανα μεσον)
3. στομα (w. δια)

## III. PREPOSITIONAL PHRASES

A. Conjunctions
   1. αχρι ου – until  Lk. 21:24

   2. αφ ου – since  Rv. 16:18

   3. ανθ ων – because  Lk. 12:3

   4. εφ ω – because  Rm. 5:12

   5. εφ οσον – inasmuch as (Mt. 25:40), as long as (Mt. 9:15)

   6. καθ οσον – inasmuch as, since – Heb. 3:3; 9:27

   7. δια τι – why  Mat. 21:25

   8. εις τι – why  Mt. 14:31

   9. εν ω – while  Lk. 5:34

B. Adverbs

   1. απο μερους – in part –  2 Co. 1:14

   2. απο ποτε – from that time on –  Mt. 4:17

   3. απ αρτι – henceforth –  Mt. 23:29

   4. δια παντος – always --  Mt. 18:10

   5. εις το παντελες – completely --  Heb. 7:25

   6. εις το παλιν – again --  2 Co. 13:13

   7. εις τον αιωνα – forever --  Jn. 6:51

8.  εν ταχει – quickly -- Ac. 12:7

9.  εν τω μεταξυ – meanwhile -- Jn. 4:31

10. εν αληθεια – sincerely, genuinely --  2 Jn. 1; 3 Jn. 1

11. επ ευλογιαις – bountifully --  2 Co. 9:6

12. κατ ιδιαν – privately --  Ac. 23:19

13. κατ αγνοιαν – ignorantly --  Ac. 3:17

## PROPER PREPOSITIONS

| PREP | ROOT IDEA | CASE | FUNCTION | MEANINGS |
|------|-----------|------|----------|----------|
| 1. ἀνά | up | acc | adv. meas. | up, in, back, again, by; each (distrib.) |
| 2. ἀντί | face to face | abl | cause, exchange | because, of |
| | | | | in exchange for, instead of, against, for |
| | | | substitution | instead of, in place of |
| 3. ἀπό | off away from | abl | separation/source | from/from |
| | | | agency/cause | by/because of, for |
| | | (gen?) | partitive | from, of |
| 4. διά | two | gen | adv. time/place | through, after/through |
| | | abl | agency/means | by/by, through |
| | | acc | cause/relation | because, for/for the benefit, sake |
| 5. εἰς | within, in | acc | adv. meas/manner | unto, for, to, among, into/in |
| | | | refer | with refer. to, about |
| | | | purpose/result | for, for purpose of/result in; so that |
| | | | cause/relation | because of/for, against |
| | | | predicate | as, to be |
| | | | spatial | into, toward, in |
| | | | temporal/advantage | for, throughout/for |
| 6. ἐκ | out of, from within | abl | separation/source | out of, away, from/from |
| | | | means/cause | by means of/ because of, result of |
| | | | temporal | from |
| | | | partitive | of |
| 7. ἐν | within | dat (?) | indir. obj./advan. | to/for |
| | | | disadv./refer | with, from/about, with ref. to |
| | | | dir. obj. | [dir. obj.] |
| | | loc | place/time/sphere | in, on, among/at, while/in, within |
| | | instr | means/cause | with, by/because of |
| | | | manner/measure | in, with/amounting to, - fold |
| | | | assoc./agency | with/by |
| | | | possession | with |
| | | | standard (=meas?) | according to |

# PROPER PREPOSITIONS (CONT.)

| PREP | ROOT IDEA | CASE | FUNCTION | MEANINGS |
|------|-----------|------|----------|----------|
| 8. ἐπί | upon | gen | adv. time/place/cause | during, at by/on, upon/ on basis of |
| | | dat | indir. obj./refer | to/about |
| | | | adv./disadv. | to, for/against, upon |
| | | loc | place/time/sphere | on, at, upon, over, before/at/in |
| | | instr(?) | cause | because of; on basis of |
| | | acc | adv. meas./relat. | upon, for, on, over/upon, against |
| | | | spatial/temporal | on, upon, against/for |
| 9. κατά | down | gen | place/oaths | throughout, upon/by |
| | | abl | source/opposition down | from/against (or gen.?) |
| | | acc | adv. refer/possess. | along, at, one (dist.)/of |
| | | | standard/spatial | in accordance with/along, at |
| | | | temporal/purpose | at/for the purpose of |
| 10. μετά | in midst of | gen | assoc./atten.cir. | with/with, among, on, to |
| | | acc | adv. measure (temp., spatial) | after, behind |
| 11. παρά | beside | abl | source/agency | from/by |
| | | loc | place/sphere | beside, with, before, near/ with in |
| | | instr(?) | assoc. | with, in presence of? |
| | | acc | adv. meas. (spatial) | beside, along |
| | | | compar./relation | …than, beyond/against, |
| | | | (opposition) | contrary to |
| 12. περί | around | gen | refer./advant. | for, about, concerning/for, in behalf of |
| | | abl(?) | purpose | for the purpose of, to… |
| | | acc | adv. meas. (spatial, temporal)/reference | around, about, near /with refer. to, with |
| 13. πρό | before | abl | separation/rank | before/above (above all) |
| | | | temp., spatial | before |
| 14. πρός | near, facing | gen | advantage (1x) | in the interest of, for (Ac. 27:34) |
| | | loc | place (6x) | at, on, near, by |
| | | acc | adv. meas.(spat, tem) | with, for, by means of (?) |
| | | | reference | w. refer. to, in accord with |
| | | | purpose/comparison | so that, for purpose of, to/ to compare with |
| | | | /result | /with the result of |
| | | | relationship (opposition) | with, against, to, at |

## PROPER PREPOSITIONS (CONT.)

| PREP | ROOT IDEA | CASE | FUNCTION | MEANINGS |
|------|-----------|------|----------|----------|
| 15. σύν | together with | instr | meas./assoc. | besides, in addition to/with together with |
| 16. ὑπέρ | over | gen | adv, refer. advantage substitution | about, as for, concerning for, for the sake of, in behalf of, instead of (substit.) |
| | | acc | comparison /spatial | more than, greater than, beyond, above, over/above, over |
| 17. ὑπό | under | abl | agency/means | by (direct) /by (impersonal) |
| | | acc | adv. measure (spatial) subordination | under, about  under |

## ASSIGNMENT

### IDENTIFY SYNTACTICAL FUNCTIONS:  PREPOSITIONS (1)

### MATTHEW 4:1-11

A.  Identify the root meaning, case and function, and resultant meaning of the preposition
    (four features)

1.  εἰς  (v.1) within/acc/advplace/into, to          7.  ἐπὶ

2.  ὑπὸ                                              8.  περὶ  (v. 6)

3.  ὑπὸ                                              9.  ἐπὶ

4.  ἐπ᾽ (v. 4)                                       10. πρὸς

5.  διὰ                                              11. εἰς  (v. 8)

6.  εἰς  (v. 5)

B.  Identify the case and its function

1.  ἡμέρας  (v. 2)                                   8.  κόσμου (v. 8)

2.  αὐτῷ  (v. 3)                                     9.  μοι (v. 9)

3.  υἱὸς                                             10. σατανα  (v. 10)

4.  ἄρτοι                                            11. κύριον

5.  θεου  (v. 4)                                     12. αὐτῷ

6.  ἀγγέλοις  (v. 6)                                 13. αὐτῷ  (v. 11)

7.  θεόν  (v. 7)

## ASSIGNMENT

### IDENTIFY SYNTACTICAL FUNCTIONS:  PREPOSITIONS (2)

**EPHESIANS 6:10-20**

A. Identify the root meaning, case and function, and resultant meaning of the preposition (four features)

| | |
|---|---|
| 1. ἐν (v. 10) | 11. ἐν |
| 2. πρὸς (v. 11) | 12. ἐν |
| 3. πρὸς | 13. εἰς |
| 4. ἐν (v. 12) | 14. ἐν |
| 5. διὰ (v. 13) | 15. περὶ |
| 6. ἐν | 16. ὑπὲρ (v. 19) |
| 7. ἐν (v. 14) | 17. ἐν (1st) |
| 8. ἐν (v. 16) | 18. ὑπὲρ (v. 20) |
| 9. ἐν | 19. ἐν (1st) |
| 10. Διὰ (v. 18) | |

B. Identify the case and its function

| | |
|---|---|
| 1. ὑμᾶς | 8. εὐαγγελίου (v. 15) |
| 2. διαβόλου | 9. εἰρήνης |
| 3. ἡμῖν (v. 12) | 10. πίστεως (v. 16) |
| 4. σκότους | 11. σωτηρίου (v. 17) |
| 5. πονηρίας | 12. θεοῦ |
| 6. θεοῦ (v. 13) | 13. στόματός (v. 19) |
| 7. δικαιοσύνης (v. 14) | 14. εὐαγγελίου |
| | 15. με (v.20) |

# LESSON SIX:
# SYMBOLISM ABOUT FAITH/SALVATION

## Vine and Branches

The vine and branches are a reminder of Jesus' teaching that believers derive life and fruitfulness from Christ, the True Vine.

## Noah's Ark

Noah's ark is symbolic of God's judgment on sin and His promise of salvation and provision for His people. It is a powerful Old Testament type of God's promised Savior, Jesus Christ.

# LESSON SIX

## READING ABOUT FAITH/SALVATION

**John 15:1** Ἐγώ εἰμι ἡ ἄμπελος ἡ ἀληθινὴ καὶ ὁ πατήρ μου ὁ γεωργός ἐστιν. **2** πᾶν κλῆμα ἐν ἐμοὶ μὴ φέρον καρπὸν αἴρει αὐτό, καὶ πᾶν τὸ καρπὸν φέρον καθαίρει αὐτὸ ἵνα καρπὸν πλείονα φέρῃ. **3** ἤδη ὑμεῖς καθαροί ἐστε διὰ τὸν λόγον ὃν λελάληκα ὑμῖν· **4** μείνατε ἐν ἐμοί, κἀγὼ ἐν ὑμῖν. καθὼς τὸ κλῆμα οὐ δύναται καρπὸν φέρειν ἀφ' ἑαυτοῦ ἐὰν μὴ μένῃ ἐν τῇ ἀμπέλῳ, οὕτως οὐδὲ ὑμεῖς ἐὰν μὴ ἐν ἐμοὶ μένητε. **5** ἐγώ εἰμι ἡ ἄμπελος, ὑμεῖς τὰ κλήματα. ὁ μένων ἐν ἐμοὶ κἀγὼ ἐν αὐτῷ οὗτος φέρει καρπὸν πολύν, ὅτι χωρὶς ἐμοῦ οὐ δύνασθε ποιεῖν οὐδέν. **6** ἐὰν μή τις μένῃ ἐν ἐμοί, ἐβλήθη ἔξω ὡς τὸ κλῆμα καὶ ἐξηράνθη καὶ συνάγουσιν αὐτὰ καὶ εἰς τὸ πῦρ βάλλουσιν καὶ καίεται. **7** ἐὰν μείνητε ἐν ἐμοὶ καὶ τὰ ῥήματά μου ἐν ὑμῖν μείνῃ, ὃ ἐὰν θέλητε αἰτήσασθε, καὶ γενήσεται ὑμῖν. **8** ἐν τούτῳ ἐδοξάσθη ὁ πατήρ μου, ἵνα καρπὸν πολὺν φέρητε καὶ γένησθε ἐμοὶ μαθηταί.

**Romans 4:1** Τί οὖν ἐροῦμεν εὑρηκέναι ᾿Αβραὰμ τὸν προπάτορα ἡμῶν κατὰ σάρκα; **2**

εἰ γὰρ ᾿Αβραὰμ ἐξ ἔργων ἐδικαιώθη, ἔχει καύχημα, ἀλλ᾿ οὐ πρὸς θεόν. **3** τί γὰρ ἡ

γραφὴ λέγει; ἐπίστευσεν δὲ ᾿Αβραὰμ τῷ θεῷ καὶ ἐλογίσθη αὐτῷ εἰς δικαιοσύνην. **4** τῷ

δὲ ἐργαζομένῳ ὁ μισθὸς οὐ λογίζεται κατὰ χάριν ἀλλὰ κατὰ ὀφείλημα, **5** τῷ δὲ μὴ

ἐργαζομένῳ πιστεύοντι δὲ ἐπὶ τὸν δικαιοῦντα τὸν ἀσεβῆ λογίζεται ἡ πίστις αὐτοῦ εἰς

δικαιοσύνην· **6** καθάπερ καὶ Δαυὶδ λέγει τὸν μακαρισμὸν τοῦ ἀνθρώπου ᾧ ὁ θεὸς

λογίζεται δικαιοσύνην χωρὶς ἔργων· **7** μακάριοι ὧν ἀφέθησαν αἱ ἀνομίαι καὶ ὧν

ἐπεκαλύφθησαν αἱ ἁμαρτίαι· **8** μακάριος ἀνὴρ οὗ οὐ μὴ λογίσηται κύριος ἁμαρτίαν. **9**

Ὁ μακαρισμὸς οὖν οὗτος ἐπὶ τὴν περιτομὴν ἢ καὶ ἐπὶ τὴν ἀκροβυστίαν; λέγομεν γάρ·

ἐλογίσθη τῷ ᾿Αβραὰμ ἡ πίστις εἰς δικαιοσύνην. **10** πῶς οὖν ἐλογίσθη; ἐν περιτομῇ

ὄντι ἢ ἐν ἀκροβυστίᾳ; οὐκ ἐν περιτομῇ ἀλλ᾿ ἐν ἀκροβυστίᾳ·


**Hebrews 11:1** Ἔστιν δὲ πίστις ἐλπιζομένων ὑπόστασις, πραγμάτων ἔλεγχος οὐ

βλεπομένων. **2** ἐν ταύτῃ γὰρ ἐμαρτυρήθησαν οἱ πρεσβύτεροι. **3** Πίστει νοοῦμεν

κατηρτίσθαι τοὺς αἰῶνας ῥήματι θεοῦ, εἰς τὸ μὴ ἐκ φαινομένων τὸ βλεπόμενον γεγονέναι. **4** Πίστει πλείονα θυσίαν Ἄβελ παρὰ Κάϊν προσήνεγκεν τῷ θεῷ, δι᾽ ἧς

ἐμαρτυρήθη εἶναι δίκαιος, μαρτυροῦντος ἐπὶ τοῖς δώροις αὐτοῦ τοῦ θεοῦ, καὶ δι᾽ αὐτῆς

ἀποθανὼν ἔτι λαλεῖ. **5** Πίστει Ἑνὼχ μετετέθη τοῦ μὴ ἰδεῖν θάνατον, καὶ οὐχ

ηὑρίσκετο διότι μετέθηκεν αὐτὸν ὁ θεός. πρὸ γὰρ τῆς μεταθέσεως μεμαρτύρηται

εὐαρεστηκέναι τῷ θεῷ· **6** χωρὶς δὲ πίστεως ἀδύνατον εὐαρεστῆσαι· πιστεῦσαι γὰρ δεῖ

τὸν προσερχόμενον τῷ θεῷ ὅτι ἔστιν καὶ τοῖς ἐκζητοῦσιν αὐτὸν μισθαποδότης γίνεται.

**7** Πίστει χρηματισθεὶς Νῶε περὶ τῶν μηδέπω βλεπομένων, εὐλαβηθεὶς κατεσκεύασεν

κιβωτὸν εἰς σωτηρίαν τοῦ οἴκου αὐτοῦ δι᾽ ἧς κατέκρινεν τὸν κόσμον, καὶ τῆς κατὰ

πίστιν δικαιοσύνης ἐγένετο κληρονόμος. **8** Πίστει καλούμενος Ἀβραὰμ ὑπήκουσεν

ἐξελθεῖν εἰς τόπον ὃν ἤμελλεν λαμβάνειν εἰς κληρονομίαν, καὶ ἐξῆλθεν μὴ ἐπιστάμενος

ποῦ ἔρχεται. **9** Πίστει παρῴκησεν εἰς γῆν τῆς ἐπαγγελίας ὡς ἀλλοτρίαν ἐν σκηναῖς

κατοικήσας μετὰ Ἰσαὰκ καὶ Ἰακὼβ τῶν συγκληρονόμων τῆς ἐπαγγελίας τῆς αὐτῆς·

**10** ἐξεδέχετο γὰρ τὴν τοὺς θεμελίους ἔχουσαν πόλιν ἧς τεχνίτης καὶ δημιουργὸς ὁ

θεός.

# QUESTIONS FOR HEART AND MIND

## FAITH/SALVATION

### ROMANS 4:1-10

1. What is Paul's purpose in citing the record of Abraham?

2. What is the key word of the passage?

3. What prompts Paul to cite the experience of David?

   How is the experience of David related to that of Abraham?

4. How does the history of Abraham support Paul's point?

   How does our history support Paul's point?

## QUESTIONS FOR HEART AND MIND

### FAITH/SALVATION

### HEBREWS 11:1-10

1.  Put verse 1 in your own words.



How does the verse reflect a biblical worldview?  That is, what constitutes reality?


How does this compare with our culture's modern worldview?



2.  What is the author's point in these verses?



3. What is the key word of this passage?        What is another key word related to the first?


4.  What is the promise (v. 9)?     Compare verses 13-16, 39-40.



How does the promise relate to us?  Why?

# CLASS DISCUSSION QUESTIONS

# ADJECTIVES; PRONOUNS

# FAITH/SALVATION

# ROMANS 4:1-10

1. What position do the words, τὸν προπάτορα ἡμῶν κατὰ σάρκα, have with respect to the word Ἀβραὰμ (v. 1)?

   What is the significance of this position?

2. Identify the following pronouns as to kind.

   Τί (v. 1)

   ἡμῶν

   αὐτῷ (v. 3)

   αὐτοῦ (v. 5)

   οὗτος (v. 9)

3. How is the adjective ἀσεβῆ used (v. 5)?

4. How are the adjectives Μακάριοι (v. 7) and μακάριος (v. 8) used?

   Why is there a change in number, from plural to singular?

   Why, do you think, did David make the change?

# CLASS DISCUSSION QUESTIONS

## ADJECTIVES; PRONOUNS

### FAITH/SALVATION

### HEBREWS 11:1-10

1. What kind of adjective is πλείονα (v. 4)?

   How is the comparison made with Κάϊν?

2. What is the position of the prepositional phrase, κατὰ πίστιν, with respect to the words, τῆς κατὰ πίστιν δικαιοσύνης (v. 7)? What is significant about this?

3. What is the adjective ἀλλοτρίαν modifying (v. 9)?

   What is the translation of this part of the verse?

4. What position does αὐτῆς have (v. 9)?

   What is the translation?

   What kind of pronoun is this word? How is it being used?

   Compare the use of the same word in verse 11. What position does it have and how is it being used?

# PRONOUNS

## I. DEFINITION

A. A pronoun sets forth the relation of a subject or object to the speaker.

B. A pronoun indicates but does not name the speaker.

C. Deictic pronouns point out, marking an object by its position in respect to the speaker; <u>anaphoric</u> pronouns refer to substantives, denoting an object already mentioned or known.

D. Pronouns stand for, are in the place of, are instead of, a noun; hence they are used much as nouns are used (similar syntax).

E. Pronouns prevent the monotony which repetition of nouns would cause.

## II. KINDS  (see B & W, 80; Wall., 315-354; charts, 320, 354)

**A. Personal** (deictic): εγω, ημεις, συ, υμεις; no third person
    1.   The nominative is used for emphasis.
    2.   The oblique cases are used as possessive, reflexive (rare) pronouns.

**B. Possessive (=adjective):** εμος, ημετερος; σος, υμετερος; ο, η, το; ιδιος

**C. Intensive** (adj. and pron.): αυτος
    1.   An adjective and pronoun
        a.  intensive adjective pronoun ("self") (predicate use)
        b.  adjective pronoun with the article ("same") (attributive use)
        c.  personal pronoun of third person in oblique cases ("him, her, it, them")
        d.  also used as possessive and demonstrative pronoun ("very, that")
    2.   Emphasizes identity

**D. Reflexive:** εμαυτου, σεατου, εαυτου; εαυτων; ιδιος

    1. Action is referred back to its own subject.
    2. The oblique case of a personal pronoun may be so used.

**E. Reciprocal:** αλληλων
    1. It expresses an interchange of action.
    2. Also a reflexive pronoun and the middle voice can be so used.

**F. Demonstrative:** ουτος, εκεινος; ο; ος; αυτος; οδε, ηδε, τοδε
  1. They are regularly placed in predicate position.
  2. They are used substantively or adjectivally.
  3. They are deictic unless without the article (then anaphoric).
  4. Sometimes ο μεν, ο δε; ος μεν, ος δε

**G. Relative** (anaphoric): ος, οστις, οσος οιος, οποιος, ηλικος
  1. Gender and number are determined by antecedent.
  2. Case is determined by the pronoun's function in its own clause.
  3. Exceptions to case form are due to attraction (direct or indirect), yet function remains.
  4. Sometimes the antecedent is omitted.

**H. Interrogative:** τις, τι; ποσος (quantity), ποιος (quality), πηλικος (quantity) ποταπος, ποτερος
  1. Used substantively (τις) or adjectively (τις ανηρ)
  2. Used in direct and in indirect questions
  3. Used adverbially ("why"); for exclamation; as relative ("what, that which"); alternatively

**I. Indefinite:** τις, τι; εις . . . εις; πας
  Used substantively ("some one") and adjectively ("some, any, certain")
  Used emphatically ("someone"), numerically; alternatively

**J. Distributive (alternative):** αλληλων, αμφοτεροι, εκαστος; αλλος, ετερος
  (adjective pronouns)

**K. Negative alternative:** ουδεις, μηδεις, ουτις, μητις; ου with πας

**L. Correlative:**     τοιουτος     ("such")---οιος, οποιος, ως, τοιοσδε ("such"); τοσουτος ("so much")---οσος; τηλικουτος ("so great")

# ASSIGNMENT

# IDENTIFY SYNTACTICAL FORMS/FUNCTIONS

# ADJECTIVES; PRONOUNS

# ROMANS 4:1-10

A. Identify the case and its function

1. Ἀβραὰμ (v. 1)

2. προπάτορα

3. ἡμῶν

4. Ἀβραὰμ (v. 2)

5. τί (v. 3)

6. γραφὴ

7. θεῷ

8. αὐτῷ

9. ἐργαζομένῳ (v. 5)

10. ἀσεβῆ

11. αὐτοῦ

12. Δαυὶδ (v. 6)

13. μακαρισμὸν

14. ἀνθρώπου

15. δικαιοσύνην

16. ἀνομίαι (v. 7)

17. ἀνὴρ (v. 8)

18. μακαρισμὸς (v. 9)

19. Ἀβραὰμ

20. πίστις

B. Identify the preposition and its function (four features)

1. κατὰ (v. 1)

2. ἐξ (v. 2)

3. πρὸς

4. εἰς (v. 3)

5. κατὰ (v. 4)

6. ἐπὶ (v. 5)

7. εἰς

8. ἐπὶ (v. 9)

9. ἐν (v. 10)

10. ἐν

## ASSIGNMENT

## IDENTIFY SYNTACTICAL FORMS/FUNCTIONS

### ADJECTIVES; PRONOUNS

### HEBREWS 11:1-10

A. Identify the case and its function

| | |
|---|---|
| 1. πίστις (v. 1) | 17. θεῷ |
| 2. ὑπόστασις | 18. προσερχόμενον (v. 6) |
| 3. πραγμάτων | 19. θεῷ |
| 4. ἔλεγχος | 20. αὐτὸν |
| 5. πρεσβύτεροι (v. 2) | 21. μισθαποδότης |
| 6. Πίστει (v. 3) | 22. κιβωτὸν (v.7) |
| 7. αἰῶνας | 23. οἴκου |
| 8. ῥήματι | 24. δικαιοσύνης |
| 9. θεοῦ | 25. κληρονόμος |
| 10. βλεπόμενον | 26. ἐπαγγελίας (v. 9) |
| 11. θυσίαν (v. 4) | 27. ἐπαγγελίας |
| 12. θεῷ | 28. θεμελίους (v. 10) |
| 13. δίκαιος | 29. πόλιν |
| 14. θεοῦ | 30. τεχνίτης |
| 15. Ἑνὼχ (v. 5) | 31. δημιουργὸς |
| 16. θάνατον | 32. θεός |

B. Identify the preposition and its function (four features)

| | |
|---|---|
| 1. ἐν (v. 2) | 8. περὶ (v. 7) |
| 2. εἰς (v. 3) | 9. εἰς |
| 3. ἐκ | 10. κατὰ |
| 4. παρὰ (v. 4) | 11. εἰς (v. 8) |
| 5. δι' (1st) | 12. εἰς |
| 6. ἐπὶ | 13. ἐν (v. 9) |
| 7  πρὸ (v. 5) | 14. μετὰ |

# LESSON SEVEN:
# SYMBOLISM ABOUT HOLINESS/HOLY SPIRIT

## Flames (Fire)

Tongues of flame, especially when shown resting on the heads of the disciples, are symbolic of the Holy Spirit and His anointing and power. Fire is also symbolic of spiritual zeal. Flames may also represent the torments of hell. When a saint is portrayed holding a flame in his or her hand, it represents religious fervor.

## Water Lily (Lotus)

Because a lotus blooms above the water from roots anchored in the mud, it is sometimes used as a symbol of the sanctifying power of Christ's Holy Spirit. It can also borrow its meaning from Greek mythology to refer to spiritual sleep or stupor.

# LESSON SEVEN

## READING ABOUT HOLINESS/HOLY SPIRIT

**John 15:9** Καθὼς ἠγάπησέν με ὁ πατήρ, κἀγὼ ὑμᾶς ἠγάπησα· μείνατε ἐν τῇ ἀγάπῃ τῇ

ἐμῇ. **10** ἐὰν τὰς ἐντολάς μου τηρήσητε, μενεῖτε ἐν τῇ ἀγάπῃ μου, καθὼς ἐγὼ τὰς

ἐντολὰς τοῦ πατρός μου τετήρηκα καὶ μένω αὐτοῦ ἐν τῇ ἀγάπῃ. **11** Ταῦτα λελάληκα

ὑμῖν ἵνα ἡ χαρὰ ἡ ἐμὴ ἐν ὑμῖν ᾖ καὶ ἡ χαρὰ ὑμῶν πληρωθῇ. **12** Αὕτη ἐστὶν ἡ ἐντολὴ

ἡ ἐμή, ἵνα ἀγαπᾶτε ἀλλήλους καθὼς ἠγάπησα ὑμᾶς. **13** μείζονα ταύτης ἀγάπην οὐδεὶς

ἔχει, ἵνα τις τὴν ψυχὴν αὐτοῦ θῇ ὑπὲρ τῶν φίλων αὐτοῦ. **14** ὑμεῖς φίλοι μού ἐστε ἐὰν

ποιῆτε ἃ ἐγὼ ἐντέλλομαι ὑμῖν. **15** οὐκέτι λέγω ὑμᾶς δούλους, ὅτι ὁ δοῦλος οὐκ οἶδεν

τί ποιεῖ αὐτοῦ ὁ κύριος· ὑμᾶς δὲ εἴρηκα φίλους, ὅτι πάντα ἃ ἤκουσα παρὰ τοῦ πατρός

μου ἐγνώρισα ὑμῖν. **16** οὐχ ὑμεῖς με ἐξελέξασθε, ἀλλ᾽ ἐγὼ ἐξελεξάμην ὑμᾶς καὶ ἔθηκα

ὑμᾶς ἵνα ὑμεῖς ὑπάγητε καὶ καρπὸν φέρητε καὶ ὁ καρπὸς ὑμῶν μένῃ, ἵνα ὅ τι ἂν

αἰτήσητε τὸν πατέρα ἐν τῷ ὀνόματί μου δῷ ὑμῖν. **17** ταῦτα ἐντέλλομαι ὑμῖν, ἵνα

ἀγαπᾶτε ἀλλήλους.

**Matthew 15:10** καὶ προσκαλεσάμενος τὸν ὄχλον εἶπεν αὐτοῖς· ἀκούετε καὶ συνίετε· **11**

οὐ τὸ εἰσερχόμενον εἰς τὸ στόμα κοινοῖ τὸν ἄνθρωπον, ἀλλὰ τὸ ἐκπορευόμενον ἐκ τοῦ

στόματος τοῦτο κοινοῖ τὸν ἄνθρωπον. **12** Τότε προσελθόντες οἱ μαθηταὶ λέγουσιν

αὐτῷ· οἶδας ὅτι οἱ Φαρισαῖοι ἀκούσαντες τὸν λόγον ἐσκανδαλίσθησαν; **13** ὁ δὲ

ἀποκριθεὶς εἶπεν· πᾶσα φυτεία ἣν οὐκ ἐφύτευσεν ὁ πατήρ μου ὁ οὐράνιος

ἐκριζωθήσεται. **14** ἄφετε αὐτούς· τυφλοί εἰσιν ὁδηγοί [τυφλῶν]· τυφλὸς δὲ τυφλὸν ἐὰν

ὁδηγῇ, ἀμφότεροι εἰς βόθυνον πεσοῦνται. **15** Ἀποκριθεὶς δὲ ὁ Πέτρος εἶπεν αὐτῷ·

φράσον ἡμῖν τὴν παραβολὴν [ταύτην]. **16** ὁ δὲ εἶπεν· ἀκμὴν καὶ ὑμεῖς ἀσύνετοί ἐστε;

**17** οὐ νοεῖτε ὅτι πᾶν τὸ εἰσπορευόμενον εἰς τὸ στόμα εἰς τὴν κοιλίαν χωρεῖ καὶ εἰς

ἀφεδρῶνα ἐκβάλλεται; **18** τὰ δὲ ἐκπορευόμενα ἐκ τοῦ στόματος ἐκ τῆς καρδίας

ἐξέρχεται, κἀκεῖνα κοινοῖ τὸν ἄνθρωπον. **19** ἐκ γὰρ τῆς καρδίας ἐξέρχονται

διαλογισμοὶ πονηροί, φόνοι, μοιχεῖαι, πορνεῖαι, κλοπαί, ψευδομαρτυρίαι, βλασφημίαι.

**20** ταῦτά ἐστιν τὰ κοινοῦντα τὸν ἄνθρωπον, τὸ δὲ ἀνίπτοις χερσὶν φαγεῖν οὐ κοινοῖ

τὸν ἄνθρωπον.

**Romans 8:5** οἱ γὰρ κατὰ σάρκα ὄντες τὰ τῆς σαρκὸς φρονοῦσιν, οἱ δὲ κατὰ πνεῦμα

τὰ τοῦ πνεύματος. **6**　τὸ γὰρ φρόνημα τῆς σαρκὸς θάνατος, τὸ δὲ φρόνημα τοῦ

πνεύματος ζωὴ καὶ εἰρήνη· **7** διότι τὸ φρόνημα τῆς σαρκὸς ἔχθρα εἰς θεόν, τῷ γὰρ

νόμῳ τοῦ θεοῦ οὐχ ὑποτάσσεται, οὐδὲ γὰρ δύναται· **8** οἱ δὲ ἐν σαρκὶ ὄντες θεῷ ἀρέσαι

οὐ δύνανται. **9** ὑμεῖς δὲ οὐκ ἐστὲ ἐν σαρκὶ ἀλλὰ ἐν πνεύματι, εἴπερ πνεῦμα θεοῦ οἰκεῖ

ἐν ὑμῖν. εἰ δέ τις πνεῦμα Χριστοῦ οὐκ ἔχει, οὗτος οὐκ ἔστιν αὐτοῦ. **10** εἰ δὲ Χριστὸς

ἐν ὑμῖν, τὸ μὲν σῶμα νεκρὸν διὰ ἁμαρτίαν τὸ δὲ πνεῦμα ζωὴ διὰ δικαιοσύνην. **11** εἰ

δὲ τὸ πνεῦμα τοῦ ἐγείραντος τὸν Ἰησοῦν ἐκ νεκρῶν οἰκεῖ ἐν ὑμῖν, ὁ ἐγείρας Χριστὸν

ἐκ νεκρῶν ζωοποιήσει καὶ τὰ θνητὰ σώματα ὑμῶν διὰ τοῦ ἐνοικοῦντος αὐτοῦ

πνεύματος ἐν ὑμῖν. **12**　Ἄρα οὖν, ἀδελφοί, ὀφειλέται ἐσμὲν οὐ τῇ σαρκὶ τοῦ κατὰ

σάρκα ζῆν, **13**　εἰ γὰρ κατὰ σάρκα ζῆτε, μέλλετε ἀποθνήσκειν· εἰ δὲ πνεύματι τὰς

πράξεις τοῦ σώματος θανατοῦτε, ζήσεσθε. **14** ὅσοι γὰρ πνεύματι θεοῦ ἄγονται, οὗτοι

υἱοὶ θεοῦ εἰσιν. **15** οὐ γὰρ ἐλάβετε πνεῦμα δουλείας πάλιν εἰς φόβον ἀλλὰ ἐλάβετε

πνεῦμα υἱοθεσίας ἐν ᾧ κράζομεν· αββα ὁ πατήρ. **16** αὐτὸ τὸ πνεῦμα συμμαρτυρεῖ τῷ πνεύματι ἡμῶν ὅτι ἐσμὲν τέκνα θεοῦ. 17 εἰ δὲ τέκνα, καὶ κληρονόμοι· κληρονόμοι μὲν

θεοῦ, συγκληρονόμοι δὲ Χριστοῦ, εἴπερ συμπάσχομεν ἵνα καὶ συνδοξασθῶμεν.

# QUESTIONS FOR HEART AND MIND

## HOLINESS/HOLY SPIRIT

## MATTHEW 15:10-20

1.  Why were the Pharisees offended (v. 12)?

2.  Why do the matters of verse 19 defile a person and not the matter of verse 20?

3.  How do the matters of verses 19-20 apply to you as a believer?

4.  How does verse 20 relate to the context?

# QUESTIONS FOR HEART AND MIND

## HOLINESS/HOLY SPIRIT

### ROMANS 8:5-17

1. How frequent are the references to the term "spirit" in this passage?

2. How is the deity of Christ implicit in 8:1-17 (vv. 3, 9)?

3. How is the deity of the Holy Spirit implicit in this passage (vv. 9, 10, 11; cf. Jn. 15:4-5)?

4. How is the Spirit connected to resurrection (v. 11)?

5. What five works of sanctification does the Holy Spirit achieve in the believer (vv. 6, 10-11, 13-16)?

6. How does sanctification take place according to the primary verse of the passage?

## CLASS DISCUSSION QUESTIONS

## THE ARTICLE

### HOLINESS/HOLY SPIRIT

### MATTHEW 15:10-20

1. What is the function of the article used with ἄνθρωπον in these verses (vv. 11, 18, 20)?

   What significance does this have?

   How does this passage impact the meaning of others where this term is used?

2. What position does the adjective οὐράνιος have in verse 13?

   What is the impact of this?

3. Note the anarthrous nouns in verse 14. What impact does the lack of the article have for the interpretation of the verse?

4. What is the use of the articles with the nouns στόμά, κοιλίαν, and καρδίας in verses 17, 18, and 19?

   What impact does this have?

5. What is significant about the anarthrous form of the plural nouns in verse 19?

   How does this form and the plurality contribute to our understanding of holiness?

# CLASS DISCUSSION QUESTIONS

## THE ARTICLE

## HOLINESS/HOLY SPIRIT

## ROMANS 8:5-17

1. What are the possible meanings for κατὰ in its two occurrences in verse 5 (cf. v. 4)?

   Are the meanings the same? Why?

2. What are the possible meanings for ἐν in verses 8-9?

   How does this preposition affect the meaning of κατὰ in verses 4-5?

   How does the middle part of verse 9 (οἰκεῖ ἐν ὑμῖν) relate to the first part?

3. How do verses 10-11 inform us of the meaning of the preceding verses? Relate this to the doctrine of the Holy Spirit.

# THE ARTICLE

## I. DEFINITIONS AND DISTINCTIVES

A. The basic function is to point out, identify, limit, make definite, define, draw attention to
   1. Substantives with the article generally are definite or generic; those without the article are indefinite or qualitative.
   2. Presence of the article emphasizes identity, the absence of the article quality

B. The article is anaphoric not deictic, hence a pointer to what is already there.

C. The article distinguishes individuals, classes, and qualities.

D. The article may be used as a pronoun: demonstrative, alternative (μεν . . . δε), relative, or possessive.

E. The article was originally a demonstrative weakened to the article or strengthened to the relative.

F. Definiteness may be accomplished by the article, use of prepositions, possessive and demonstrative pronouns, and the genitive case.

G. The article may be in the attributive or predicate position with respect to an adjective, or be repeated.

## II. USES (see B & W, 73-79; Wallace, with charts, 255-290)

A. **Identify:** to identify or denote persons or things: το ορος (Mt. 5:1)

B. **Monadic:** to indicate that a substantive is unique: τον κοσμον (Jn. 3:16)

C. **Anaphoric:** to denote previous reference: τους μαγους (Mt. 2:7)

D. **Abstract:** to distinguish one quality from another: η αγαπη (1 Cor. 13:4)
   1. It objectifies or personifies an abstract noun
   2. It is usually not translated

E. **Proper name:** to emphasize a proper name (occasional): τον θεον (Ac. 15:19)

F. **Generic:** to distinguish one class or group from another; to show something to be typical or representative of a class or group (translated often as indefinite or as plural): ο εθνικος (Mt. 18:17)

G. **Granville-Sharp rule:** to indicate that substantives in the same case connected by kai have a special relationship (see Wall., 270-90):
τον μεγαλου Θεου και σωτηρος ημων Ιησου χριστου (Titus 2:13; cf. Jn. 20:17; 2 Cor.1:3; 1 Thes. 3:2; Heb. 12:2; 2 Pet. 1:1, 11; 2:20; 3:18; Rev. 1:9)

H. **Pronomial**
   1. Demonstrative ("this, that; these those"): οι (Heb. 13:24)
   2. Personal ("he, she, they"—nominative case): ο (Mt. 13:29)
   3. Alternative:    ο μεν, ο δε; οι μεν, οι δε ("one...another"; "some...others") (1 Cor. 7:7)
   4. Possessive: τον αδελφον (2 Cor. 8:18)
   5. Relative (repetition of the article in a phrase modifying an articular substantive): πιστει τη (1 Tim. 3:13)

I. **Colwell's rule**: to distinguish the subject nominative (articular) from a definite predicate nominative (anarthrous) in a sentence having a linking verb (cf. Wall., 256-270): ο θεος αγαπη εστιν    (1  John  4:8;  Mk.  15:36;  cf.  Jn.  1:1: θεος ην ο λογος)

J. **Functional (Bracket use):** To indicate the grammatical function or relationships of indeclinable nouns, participles, infinitives, prepositional phrases, adjectival clauses and modifiers (usually untranslated). The article is used with parts of speech other than a noun: τον απο Ναζαρετ (Jn. 1:45); των δυο (Ac. 1:24); το της δοξης και το του θεου πνευμα (1 Peter 4:14).

K. **Substitutional:** to take the place of a noun, when it stands with words or phrases which modify the omitted noun: τα εν τω κοσμω (I John 2:15)

## ASSIGNMENT

## IDENTIFY SYNTACTICAL FUNCTIONS

### THE ARTICLE

### MATTHEW 15:10-20

A.  Identify the use of the article

1.  τὸν  (v. 10)                           11. ὁ  (v. 15)

2.  τὸ  (1ˢᵗ) (v. 11)                      12. τὴν

3.  τὸ  (2ⁿᵈ)                              13. ὁ  (v. 16)

4.  τοῦ                                    14. τὸ  (1ˢᵗ) (v. 17)

5.  τὸν                                    15. τὸ  (2ⁿᵈ)

6.  οἱ  (1ˢᵗ) (v. 12)                      16. τὴν

7.  οἱ  (2ⁿᵈ)                              17. τῆς  (v. 18)

8.  τὸν                                    18. τὸν

9.  ὁ  (1ˢᵗ) (v. 13)                       19. τὰ  (v. 20)

10. ὁ  (2ⁿᵈ)                               20. τὸ

B.  Identify the case and its function

1.  τὸ εἰσερχόμενον  (v. 11)               6.  ἀσύνετοί  (v. 16)

2.  τοῦτο                                  7.  κἀκεῖνα  (v. 18)

3.  φυτεία  (v. 13)                        8.  διαλογισμοὶ  (v. 19)

4.  [τυφλῶν]  (v. 14)                      9.  χερσὶν  (v. 20)

5.  ἡμῖν  (v. 15)                          10. τὸ φαγεῖν

# ASSIGNMENT

## IDENTIFY SYNTACTICAL FUNCTIONS

### THE ARTICLE

### ROMANS 8:5-17

A. Identify the use of the article

1. οἱ (v. 5)

2. τὰ

3. τῆς

4. οἱ

5. τὸ (v. 7)

6. τῷ

7. τοῦ

8. τὸ (1ˢᵗ) (v. 10)

9. τὸ (2ⁿᵈ)

10. τοῦ (v. 11)

11. τὸν

12. ὁ

13. τοῦ

14. τῇ (v. 12)

15. τοῦ

16. τὰς (v. 13)

17. τοῦ

18. ὁ (v. 15)

19. τὸ (v. 16)

20. τῷ

B. Identify the case and its function

1. σαρκὸς (v. 5)

2. σαρκὸς (v. 6)

3. θάνατος

4. νόμῳ (v. 7)

5. θεοῦ

6. θεῷ (v. 8)

7. σαρκὶ (v. 9)

8. θεοῦ

9. Χριστοῦ

10. αὐτου

11. νεκρὸν (v. 10)

12. Ἰησοῦν (v. 11)

13. ὑμῖν

14. σώματα

15. πνεύματος

16. ἀδελφοι (v. 12)

17. ὀφειλέται

18. σαρκὶ

19. πνεύματι (v. 13)

20. σώματος

21. πνεύματι (v. 14)

22. θεοῦ

23. δουλείας (v. 15)

24. υἱοθεσία

25. αββα

26. πατήρ

27. πνεύματι (v. 16)

28. Χριστοῦ (v. 17)

# LESSON EIGHT:
# SYMBOLISM ABOUT THE CHURCH

## Beehive

The beehive is a relatively modern symbol representing the church. Many bees, each assigned a different task, working together for the building up of the hive reminded artists of the Body of Christ, which is built up (edified) by many believers with differing spiritual gifts. The beehive may also be used as an emblem of St. Bernard of Clairveaux, and of St. Ambrose, who is the patron saint of beekeepers.

# LESSON EIGHT

## READING ABOUT THE CHURCH

**John 15:18** Εἰ ὁ κόσμος ὑμᾶς μισεῖ, γινώσκετε ὅτι ἐμὲ πρῶτον ὑμῶν μεμίσηκεν. 19

εἰ ἐκ τοῦ κόσμου ἦτε, ὁ κόσμος ἂν τὸ ἴδιον ἐφίλει· ὅτι δὲ ἐκ τοῦ κόσμου οὐκ ἐστέ,

ἀλλ᾽ ἐγὼ ἐξελεξάμην ὑμᾶς ἐκ τοῦ κόσμου, διὰ τοῦτο μισεῖ ὑμᾶς ὁ κόσμος. 20

μνημονεύετε τοῦ λόγου οὗ ἐγὼ εἶπον ὑμῖν· οὐκ ἔστιν δοῦλος μείζων τοῦ κυρίου αὐτοῦ.

εἰ ἐμὲ ἐδίωξαν, καὶ ὑμᾶς διώξουσιν· εἰ τὸν λόγον μου ἐτήρησαν, καὶ τὸν ὑμέτερον

τηρήσουσιν. 21 ἀλλὰ ταῦτα πάντα ποιήσουσιν εἰς ὑμᾶς διὰ τὸ ὄνομά μου, ὅτι οὐκ

οἴδασιν τὸν πέμψαντά με. 22 εἰ μὴ ἦλθον καὶ ἐλάλησα αὐτοῖς, ἁμαρτίαν οὐκ εἴχοσαν·

νῦν δὲ πρόφασιν οὐκ ἔχουσιν περὶ τῆς ἁμαρτίας αὐτῶν. 23 ὁ ἐμὲ μισῶν καὶ τὸν

πατέρα μου μισεῖ. 24 εἰ τὰ ἔργα μὴ ἐποίησα ἐν αὐτοῖς ἃ οὐδεὶς ἄλλος ἐποίησεν,

ἁμαρτίαν οὐκ εἴχοσαν· νῦν δὲ καὶ ἑωράκασιν καὶ μεμισήκασιν καὶ ἐμὲ καὶ τὸν πατέρα

μου. 25 ἀλλ᾽ ἵνα πληρωθῇ ὁ λόγος ὁ ἐν τῷ νόμῳ αὐτῶν γεγραμμένος ὅτι ἐμίσησάν με

δωρεάν. 26 Ὅταν ἔλθῃ ὁ παράκλητος ὃν ἐγὼ πέμψω ὑμῖν παρὰ τοῦ πατρός, τὸ πνεῦμα τῆς ἀληθείας ὃ παρὰ τοῦ πατρὸς ἐκπορεύεται, ἐκεῖνος μαρτυρήσει περὶ ἐμοῦ· 27 καὶ

ὑμεῖς δὲ μαρτυρεῖτε, ὅτι ἀπ᾽ ἀρχῆς μετ᾽ ἐμοῦ ἐστε.

**Colossians 3:5** Νεκρώσατε οὖν τὰ μέλη τὰ ἐπὶ τῆς γῆς, πορνείαν ἀκαθαρσίαν πάθος

ἐπιθυμίαν κακήν, καὶ τὴν πλεονεξίαν, ἥτις ἐστὶν εἰδωλολατρία, 6 δι᾽ ἃ ἔρχεται ἡ ὀργὴ

τοῦ θεοῦ [ἐπὶ τοὺς υἱοὺς τῆς ἀπειθείας]. 7 ἐν οἷς καὶ ὑμεῖς περιεπατήσατέ ποτε, ὅτε

ἐζῆτε ἐν τούτοις· 8 νυνὶ δὲ ἀπόθεσθε καὶ ὑμεῖς τὰ πάντα, ὀργήν, θυμόν, κακίαν,

βλασφημίαν, αἰσχρολογίαν ἐκ τοῦ στόματος ὑμῶν· 9 μὴ ψεύδεσθε εἰς ἀλλήλους,

ἀπεκδυσάμενοι τὸν παλαιὸν ἄνθρωπον σὺν ταῖς πράξεσιν αὐτοῦ 10 καὶ ἐνδυσάμενοι

τὸν νέον τὸν ἀνακαινούμενον εἰς ἐπίγνωσιν κατ᾽ εἰκόνα τοῦ κτίσαντος αὐτόν, 11 ὅπου

οὐκ ἔνι Ἕλλην καὶ Ἰουδαῖος, περιτομὴ καὶ ἀκροβυστία, βάρβαρος, Σκύθης, δοῦλος,

ἐλεύθερος, ἀλλὰ [τὰ] πάντα καὶ ἐν πᾶσιν Χριστός. 12 Ἐνδύσασθε οὖν, ὡς ἐκλεκτοὶ τοῦ

θεοῦ ἅγιοι καὶ ἠγαπημένοι, σπλάγχνα οἰκτιρμοῦ χρηστότητα ταπεινοφροσύνην πραΰτητα

μακροθυμίαν, 13 ἀνεχόμενοι ἀλλήλων καὶ χαριζόμενοι ἑαυτοῖς ἐάν τις πρός τινα ἔχῃ

μομφήν· καθὼς καὶ ὁ κύριος ἐχαρίσατο ὑμῖν, οὕτως καὶ ὑμεῖς· 14 ἐπὶ πᾶσιν δὲ τούτοις

τὴν ἀγάπην, ὅ ἐστιν σύνδεσμος τῆς τελειότητος. 15 καὶ ἡ εἰρήνη τοῦ Χριστοῦ βραβευέτω ἐν ταῖς καρδίαις ὑμῶν, εἰς ἣν καὶ ἐκλήθητε ἐν ἑνὶ σώματι· καὶ εὐχάριστοι

γίνεσθε. **16** Ὁ λόγος τοῦ Χριστοῦ ἐνοικείτω ἐν ὑμῖν πλουσίως, ἐν πάσῃ σοφίᾳ

διδάσκοντες καὶ νουθετοῦντες ἑαυτούς, ψαλμοῖς ὕμνοις ᾠδαῖς πνευματικαῖς ἐν [τῇ]

χάριτι ᾄδοντες ἐν ταῖς καρδίαις ὑμῶν τῷ θεῷ· **17** καὶ πᾶν ὅ τι ἐὰν ποιῆτε ἐν λόγῳ ἢ

ἐν ἔργῳ, πάντα ἐν ὀνόματι κυρίου Ἰησοῦ, εὐχαριστοῦντες τῷ θεῷ πατρὶ δι' αὐτοῦ.


**1 Corinthians 14:26** Τί οὖν ἐστιν, ἀδελφοί; ὅταν συνέρχησθε, ἕκαστος ψαλμὸν ἔχει,

διδαχὴν ἔχει, ἀποκάλυψιν ἔχει, γλῶσσαν ἔχει, ἑρμηνείαν ἔχει· πάντα πρὸς οἰκοδομὴν

γινέσθω. **27** εἴτε γλώσσῃ τις λαλεῖ, κατὰ δύο ἢ τὸ πλεῖστον τρεῖς καὶ ἀνὰ μέρος, καὶ

εἷς διερμηνευέτω· **28** ἐὰν δὲ μὴ ᾖ διερμηνευτής, σιγάτω ἐν ἐκκλησίᾳ, ἑαυτῷ δὲ

λαλείτω καὶ τῷ θεῷ. **29** προφῆται δὲ δύο ἢ τρεῖς λαλείτωσαν καὶ οἱ ἄλλοι

διακρινέτωσαν· **30** ἐὰν δὲ ἄλλῳ ἀποκαλυφθῇ καθημένῳ, ὁ πρῶτος σιγάτω. **31** δύνασθε

γὰρ καθ' ἕνα πάντες προφητεύειν, ἵνα πάντες μανθάνωσιν καὶ πάντες παρακαλῶνται.

**32** καὶ πνεύματα προφητῶν προφήταις ὑποτάσσεται, **33** οὐ γάρ ἐστιν ἀκαταστασίας ὁ

θεὸς ἀλλὰ εἰρήνης. Ὡς ἐν πάσαις ταῖς ἐκκλησίαις τῶν ἁγίων **34** αἱ γυναῖκες ἐν ταῖς ἐκκλησίαις σιγάτωσαν· οὐ γὰρ ἐπιτρέπεται αὐταῖς λαλεῖν, ἀλλὰ ὑποτασσέσθωσαν, καθὼς

καὶ ὁ νόμος λέγει. **35** εἰ δέ τι μαθεῖν θέλουσιν, ἐν οἴκῳ τοὺς ἰδίους ἄνδρας

ἐπερωτάτωσαν· αἰσχρὸν γάρ ἐστιν γυναικὶ λαλεῖν ἐν ἐκκλησίᾳ. **36** ἢ ἀφ' ὑμῶν ὁ λόγος

τοῦ θεοῦ ἐξῆλθεν, ἢ εἰς ὑμᾶς μόνους κατήντησεν;

# QUESTIONS FOR HEART AND MIND

## THE CHURCH

### COLOSSIANS 3:5-17

1.  What is the grammatical indicator, and what is the theological idea, that show how verses 5ff. are connected to the preceding verses?

    Similarly, how are verses 12ff. connected to the preceding?

2.  What are the indicators that verses 12ff. can be appropriately understood as addressing the believers gathered in community?

3.  What traits does Paul desire for a Christian community?

    What resources are at the disposal of such a community?

    How does Paul make love preeminent?

4.  According to verse 16, what role do psalms, hymns, and spiritual songs have in worship in the community?  That is, do they belong to the instruction or to the singing?

5.  What command in Ephesians parallels the command in verse 16?

# QUESTIONS FOR HEART AND MIND

## THE CHURCH

### 1 CORINTHIANS 14:26-36

1. What does this passage tell us about the variety of spiritual gifts at Corinth?

2. What is Paul's chief concern about the exercise of spiritual gifts?

3. Are verses 27-30 normative (standards or limits for the contemporary church)?

4. How can we reconcile verses 34-35 with chapter 11 and 1 Timothy 2:12-15?

5. What principles should be derived from this passage?

6. What applications does Paul make?

7. What does Paul believe about the gift of prophecy?  Is it still operative?

# CLASS DISCUSSION QUESTIONS

## REVIEW OF SYNTAX

## THE CHURCH

## COLOSSIANS 3:5-17

1. What is the emphasis resulting from the repetition of the article τά in verse 5?

2. What is the import of the anarthrous form of the first four and sixth vices, but the articular form of the fifth one (v. 5)?

3. In what case is each of the vices, and what is the function involved (v. 5)?

4. What are the options for the function of the form θεοῦ (v. 6)?

5. What is the function of the case involved in τοῦ κτίσαντος (v. 10)?

6. What is the import of the anarthrous form of the nouns in verse 11? Of such nouns in verse 12?

7. In what ways is the place of love in the community emphasized (v. 14)?

8. What are the options for the function of the case in Χριστοῦ (v. 16)?

9. How does one resolve whether the "teaching and admonishing" or the "singing" is to be done by "psalms, hymns, spiritual songs" (v. 16)?

10. What is the impact of the asyndeton found in verses 5, 8, 12, 16? Compare verse 11.

## CLASS DISCUSSION QUESTIONS

### REVIEW OF SYNTAX

### THE CHURCH

### I CORINTHIANS 14:26-36

1.  In light of this passage, is any one of the gifts gender specific?  Compare verses 26, 34-35?

2.  Is Paul's restriction regarding "two or three" speakers in tongues and "two or three" prophets prophesying absolute and normative, or descriptive?  What in the text or context (including background) helps to resolve this?

3.  Is Paul's chief concern in this passage to instruct on certain gifts, or is his concern broader?   In what ways is this made apparent?

4.  What is the import of the anarthrous form of the nouns (v. 26)?

5.  What are the options for the function of the case involved in προφητῶν (v. 32)?

6.  What are the options for the function of the case involved in θεοῦ (v. 36)?

## ASSIGNMENT

## IDENTIFY SYNTACTICAL FORMS/FUNCTIONS

## CASE, PREPOSITION, ARTICLE

### 1 CORINTHIANS 14:26-36

A.  Identify the case and its function

1.  Τί (v. 26)
2.  ἕκαστος
3.  πάντα
4.  γλώσσῃ (v. 27)
5.  διερμηνευτής (v. 28)
6.  ἑαυτῷ
7.  προφῆται (v. 29)
8.  ἄλλῳ (v. 30)
9.  πάντες (v. 31)
10. πνεύματα (v. 32)

11. προφητῶν
12. προφήταις
13. ἀκαταστασίας (v. 33)
14. θεὸς
15. ἁγίων
16. γυναῖκες (v. 34)
17. αὐταῖς
18. τι (v. 35)
19. γυναικὶ
20. θεοῦ (v. 36)

B.  Identify the function of the preposition (four features)

1.  πρὸς (v. 26)
2.  κατὰ (v. 27)
3.  ἀνὰ
4.  ἐν (v. 28)
5.  καθ' (v. 31)

6.  ἐν (v. 33)
7.  ἐν (v. 35)
8.  ἐν
9.  ἀφ' (v. 36)
10. εἰς

C.  Identify the function of the article

1.  τὸ (v. 27)
2.  τῷ (v. 28)
3.  οἱ (v. 29)
4.  ὁ (v. 30)
5.  ὁ (v. 33)
6.  ταῖς

7.  τῶν
8.  αἱ (v. 34)
9.  ὁ
10. τοὺς (v. 35)
11. ὁ (v. 36)
12. τοῦ

## ASSIGNMENT
# IDENTIFY SYNTACTICAL FORMS/FUNCTIONS
### CASE, PREPOSITION, ARTICLE
### COLOSSIANS 3:5-17

A. Identify the case and its function
1. μέλη (v. 5)
2. πορνείαν
3. εἰδωλολατρία
4. ὀργήν (v. 8)
5. κτίσαντος (v. 10)
6. αὐτόν
7. Ἕλλην (v. 11)
8. πάντα
9. Χριστός
10. ἐκλεκτοὶ (v. 12)
11. θεοῦ
12. σπλάγχνα
13. ἑαυτοῖς (v. 13)
14. ὑμῖν
15. σύνδεσμος (v. 14)
16. τελειότητος
17. Χριστοῦ (v. 15)
18. Χριστοῦ (v. 16)
19. ψαλμοῖς
20. θεῷ
21. πάντα (v. 17)
22. πατρὶ

B. Identify the function of the preposition (four elements)
1. ἐπι (v. 5)
2. δι' (v. 6)
3. ἐν (v. 7)
4. ἐκ (v. 8)
5. εἰς (v. 9)
6. σὺν
7. κατ' (v. 10)
8. ἐν (v. 11)
9. πρός (v. 13)
10. ἐπὶ (v. 14)
11. ἐν (2nd) (v. 16)
12. δι' (v. 17)

C. Identify the function of the article
1. τὰ (1st) (v. 5)
2. τὰ (2nd)
3. τῆς
4. τὴν
5. ἡ (v. 6)
6. τοῦ
7. τοὺς
8. τῆς
9. τὰ (v. 8)
10. τοῦ
11. τὸν (v. 9)
12. τὸν (2nd) (v. 10)
13. τοῦ
14. ὁ (v. 13)
15. τὴν (v. 14)
16. τῆς
17. ἡ (v. 15)
18. τοῦ
19. ταῖς
20. ὁ (v. 16)

# LESSON NINE:
## SYMBOLISM ABOUT SIN/HUMANITY

### Thistle

The thistle is a symbol of temporal sorrow and the curse of sin from the story of the Fall. Because the thistle is a thorny bush, it is often portrayed as the source of Christ's crown of thorns. Because thistles flourish to crowd out useful crops, they have also been used to represent the "tares" or weeds written of in Matthew 13.

## LESSON NINE

### READING ABOUT SIN/HUMANITY

**John 16:1** Ταῦτα λελάληκα ὑμῖν ἵνα μὴ σκανδαλισθῆτε. **2** ἀποσυναγώγους ποιήσουσιν

ὑμᾶς· ἀλλ' ἔρχεται ὥρα ἵνα πᾶς ὁ ἀποκτείνας ὑμᾶς δόξῃ λατρείαν προσφέρειν τῷ θεῷ.

**3** καὶ ταῦτα ποιήσουσιν ὅτι οὐκ ἔγνωσαν τὸν πατέρα οὐδὲ ἐμέ. **4** ἀλλὰ ταῦτα

λελάληκα ὑμῖν ἵνα ὅταν ἔλθῃ ἡ ὥρα αὐτῶν μνημονεύητε αὐτῶν ὅτι ἐγὼ εἶπον ὑμῖν.

Ταῦτα δὲ ὑμῖν ἐξ ἀρχῆς οὐκ εἶπον, ὅτι μεθ' ὑμῶν ἤμην. **5** Νῦν δὲ ὑπάγω πρὸς τὸν

πέμψαντά με, καὶ οὐδεὶς ἐξ ὑμῶν ἐρωτᾷ με· ποῦ ὑπάγεις; **6** ἀλλ' ὅτι ταῦτα λελάληκα

ὑμῖν ἡ λύπη πεπλήρωκεν ὑμῶν τὴν καρδίαν. **7** ἀλλ' ἐγὼ τὴν ἀλήθειαν λέγω ὑμῖν,

συμφέρει ὑμῖν ἵνα ἐγὼ ἀπέλθω. ἐὰν γὰρ μὴ ἀπέλθω, ὁ παράκλητος οὐκ ἐλεύσεται πρὸς

ὑμᾶς· ἐὰν δὲ πορευθῶ, πέμψω αὐτὸν πρὸς ὑμᾶς. **8** καὶ ἐλθὼν ἐκεῖνος ἐλέγξει τὸν

κόσμον περὶ ἁμαρτίας καὶ περὶ δικαιοσύνης καὶ περὶ κρίσεως· **9** περὶ ἁμαρτίας μέν,

ὅτι οὐ πιστεύουσιν εἰς ἐμέ· **10** περὶ δικαιοσύνης δέ, ὅτι πρὸς τὸν πατέρα ὑπάγω καὶ

οὐκέτι θεωρεῖτέ με· **11** περὶ δὲ κρίσεως, ὅτι ὁ ἄρχων τοῦ κόσμου τούτου κέκριται.

**John 9:24** Ἐφώνησαν οὖν τὸν ἄνθρωπον ἐκ δευτέρου ὃς ἦν τυφλὸς καὶ εἶπαν αὐτῷ·

δὸς δόξαν τῷ θεῷ· ἡμεῖς οἴδαμεν ὅτι οὗτος ὁ ἄνθρωπος ἁμαρτωλός ἐστιν. **25** ἀπεκρίθη

οὖν ἐκεῖνος· εἰ ἁμαρτωλός ἐστιν οὐκ οἶδα· ἓν οἶδα ὅτι τυφλὸς ὢν ἄρτι βλέπω. **26**

εἶπον οὖν αὐτῷ· τί ἐποίησέν σοι; πῶς ἤνοιξέν σου τοὺς ὀφθαλμούς; **27** ἀπεκρίθη

αὐτοῖς· εἶπον ὑμῖν ἤδη καὶ οὐκ ἠκούσατε· τί πάλιν θέλετε ἀκούειν; μὴ καὶ ὑμεῖς θέλετε

αὐτοῦ μαθηταὶ γενέσθαι; **28** καὶ ἐλοιδόρησαν αὐτὸν καὶ εἶπον· σὺ μαθητὴς εἶ ἐκείνου,

ἡμεῖς δὲ τοῦ Μωϋσέως ἐσμὲν μαθηταί· **29** ἡμεῖς οἴδαμεν ὅτι Μωϋσεῖ λελάληκεν ὁ

θεός, τοῦτον δὲ οὐκ οἴδαμεν πόθεν ἐστίν. **30** ἀπεκρίθη ὁ ἄνθρωπος καὶ εἶπεν αὐτοῖς·

ἐν τούτῳ γὰρ τὸ θαυμαστόν ἐστιν, ὅτι ὑμεῖς οὐκ οἴδατε πόθεν ἐστίν, καὶ ἤνοιξέν μου

τοὺς ὀφθαλμούς. **31** οἴδαμεν ὅτι ἁμαρτωλῶν ὁ θεὸς οὐκ ἀκούει, ἀλλ' ἐάν τις θεοσεβὴς

ᾖ καὶ τὸ θέλημα αὐτοῦ ποιῇ τούτου ἀκούει. **32** ἐκ τοῦ αἰῶνος οὐκ ἠκούσθη ὅτι

ἠνέῳξέν τις ὀφθαλμοὺς τυφλοῦ γεγεννημένου· **33** εἰ μὴ ἦν οὗτος παρὰ θεοῦ, οὐκ

ἠδύνατο ποιεῖν οὐδέν. **34** ἀπεκρίθησαν καὶ εἶπαν αὐτῷ· ἐν ἁμαρτίαις σὺ ἐγεννήθης

ὅλος καὶ σὺ διδάσκεις ἡμᾶς; καὶ ἐξέβαλον αὐτὸν ἔξω.

**John 9:40** ἤκουσαν ἐκ τῶν Φαρισαίων ταῦτα οἱ μετ' αὐτοῦ ὄντες καὶ εἶπον αὐτῷ· μὴ

καὶ ἡμεῖς τυφλοί ἐσμεν; **41** εἶπεν αὐτοῖς ὁ Ἰησοῦς· εἰ τυφλοὶ ἦτε, οὐκ ἂν εἴχετε

ἁμαρτίαν· νῦν δὲ λέγετε ὅτι βλέπομεν, ἡ ἁμαρτία ὑμῶν μένει.

**Hebrews 2:5** Οὐ γὰρ ἀγγέλοις ὑπέταξεν τὴν οἰκουμένην τὴν μέλλουσαν, περὶ ἧς

λαλοῦμεν. **6** διεμαρτύρατο δέ πού τις λέγων· τί ἐστιν ἄνθρωπος ὅτι μιμνῄσκῃ αὐτοῦ, ἢ

υἱὸς ἀνθρώπου ὅτι ἐπισκέπτῃ αὐτόν; **7** ἠλάττωσας αὐτὸν βραχύ τι παρ' ἀγγέλους, δόξῃ

καὶ τιμῇ ἐστεφάνωσας αὐτόν, **8** πάντα ὑπέταξας ὑποκάτω τῶν ποδῶν αὐτοῦ. ἐν τῷ γὰρ

ὑποτάξαι [αὐτῷ] τὰ πάντα οὐδὲν ἀφῆκεν αὐτῷ ἀνυπότακτον. Νῦν δὲ οὔπω ὁρῶμεν αὐτῷ

τὰ πάντα ὑποτεταγμένα· **9** τὸν δὲ βραχύ τι παρ' ἀγγέλους ἠλαττωμένον βλέπομεν

Ἰησοῦν διὰ τὸ πάθημα τοῦ θανάτου δόξῃ καὶ τιμῇ ἐστεφανωμένον, ὅπως χάριτι θεοῦ

ὑπὲρ παντὸς γεύσηται θανάτου. **10** ἔπρεπεν γὰρ αὐτῷ, δι' ὃν τὰ πάντα καὶ δι' οὗ τὰ

πάντα, πολλοὺς υἱοὺς εἰς δόξαν ἀγαγόντα τὸν ἀρχηγὸν τῆς σωτηρίας αὐτῶν διὰ

παθημάτων τελειῶσαι. **11** ὅ τε γὰρ ἁγιάζων καὶ οἱ ἁγιαζόμενοι ἐξ ἑνὸς πάντες· δι' ἣν

αἰτίαν οὐκ ἐπαισχύνεται ἀδελφοὺς αὐτοὺς καλεῖν **12** λέγων· ἀπαγγελῶ τὸ ὄνομά σου τοῖς ἀδελφοῖς μου, ἐν μέσῳ ἐκκλησίας ὑμνήσω σε, 13 καὶ πάλιν· ἐγὼ ἔσομαι πεποιθὼς

ἐπ᾽ αὐτῷ, καὶ πάλιν· ἰδοὺ ἐγὼ καὶ τὰ παιδία ἅ μοι ἔδωκεν ὁ θεός. 14 Ἐπεὶ οὖν τὰ

παιδία κεκοινώνηκεν αἵματος καὶ σαρκός, καὶ αὐτὸς παραπλησίως μετέσχεν τῶν αὐτῶν,

ἵνα διὰ τοῦ θανάτου καταργήσῃ τὸν τὸ κράτος ἔχοντα τοῦ θανάτου, τοῦτ᾽ ἔστιν τὸν

διάβολον, 15 καὶ ἀπαλλάξῃ τούτους, ὅσοι φόβῳ θανάτου διὰ παντὸς τοῦ ζῆν ἔνοχοι

ἦσαν δουλείας. 16 οὐ γὰρ δήπου ἀγγέλων ἐπιλαμβάνεται ἀλλὰ σπέρματος Ἀβραὰμ

ἐπιλαμβάνεται.

# QUESTIONS FOR HEART AND MIND

## SIN/HUMANITY

### JOHN 9:24-34, 40-41

1.  What made the blind man a sinner in the eyes of the disciples?

2.  What made Christ a sinner in the eyes of the Pharisees?

3.  What made the Pharisees sinners in the eyes of Christ?

4.  What was the purpose of the blindness of the man?

5.  What truly makes one a sinner according to this passage?

6.  What does this passage teach us about the nature of sin?

# QUESTIONS FOR HEART AND MIND

## SIN/HUMANITY

### HEBREWS 2:5-16

1. List four ways by which human beings are exalted in this passage.

2. Why is the name Ἰησοῦν used in verse 9?

3. Why is Jesus our brother (vv. 11 ff.)?

4. Why did Christ become "blood and flesh" (vv. 14 ff.)?

5. List four things about the nature of human beings.

# CLASS DISCUSSION QUESTIONS

## VOICE

## SIN/HUMANITY

### HEBREWS 2:5-16

1.    What is the voice of ἁγιαζόμενοι in verse 11?


      What is the meaning if it were middle?


      What is the meaning if it were passive?


2.    If the form is passive, who is the agent doing the action?


      Consider your answer in light of the subject (doer) of ἁγιάζων.  Are the subjects the same?


3.    Who is the referent of ἑνὸς?


4.    How does the voice of these terms (in v. 11) contribute to the doctrine of sanctification?


      How does the tense contribute to this doctrine?


5.    What in verse 11a allows for the substantiation or assertion of 11b?  That is, what is the referent of ἣν αἰτίαν in verse 11?

# CLASS DISCUSSION QUESTIONS

## MOOD

## SIN/HUMANITY

## JOHN 9:24-34, 40-41

1.  What mood is employed in ᾖ and ποιῇ (9:31)?

2.  What is the significance of the mood in general?

3.  What is the significance of this mood here? How does it fit the context?

4.  What is the logic or conclusion of the blind man's observation or universal principle as applied to Christ?

# VOICE
## (Relation of Subject to Verb)

| Function | Key Concepts | N.T. Example | B&W | Wall |
|---|---|---|---|---|
| **A. ACTIVE  (Subject Produces Action)** | | | | |
| 1. Simple | Subj. produces action | Lk.22:54; 1 Cor.3:6 | 110 | 411 |
| 2. Causative | Subj. causes action | 1 Cor. 3:6; Ac. 13:19 | 110 | 411 |
| 3. Stative | Equative verb or idea | Jn.1:1; 1 Cor.13:4 | -- | 412 |
| **B. MIDDLE  (Subject Participates)** | | | | |
| 1. Direct | Reflexive | Mk.7:4; Mt.27:5 | 111 | 416 |
| 2. Indirect | Intensive | 1 Cor.13:8; 2 Tim.4:15 | 111 | 419 |
| 3. Permissive | "Permit; cause" | Lk.2:4,5; 1 Cor.6:7 | 112 | 425 |
| 4. Reciprocal | Plural Subject | Mt.26:4; Jn.9:22 | 113 | 427 |
| 5. Deponent | Middle form, active meaning | | -- | 428 |
| **C. PASSIVE  (Subject Acted Upon)** | | | | |
| 1. Direct | Orig. Agent (cf. υπο) | Ac.22:30; Mt.10:22 | 103 | 433 |
| 2. Intermediate | Medium (cf. δια) | Jn.1:3; Mt.1:22 | -- | 433 |
| 3. Impersonal | Instrument (cf. εν, εκ) | Eph.2:8; Mt.3:12 | -- | 434 |

# MOOD
## (Manner of Affirmation; Relation to Reality)

### A.  INDICATIVE  (Affirms Reality)

| | | | | |
|---|---|---|---|---|
| 1. Declarative | States Fact (also 1$^{st}$ class cond) | Eph.4:1; Jn.1:1 | 114 | 449 |
| 2. Interrogative | Question | Mt.16:13; Mk.1:24 | 115 | 449 |
| 3. Potential | Contingency | | | |
|    a. Cohortative | Command (future) | Lk.1:13; Jas.2:8 | 115 | 451 |
|    b. Obligation | Necessity, Possibility | Mt.25:27; Ac.17:29 | 116 | 451 |
|    c. Impulse | Wish | Ac.25:22; Gal.5:12 | 116 | 451 |
|    d. Condition | Second class | Ac. 26:32; Lk.7:39 | 117 | 450 |

### B.  SUBJUNCTIVE  (Probability)

| | | | | |
|---|---|---|---|---|
| 1. Hortatory | "Let Us" | Heb.12:1; 1 Jn.4:7 | 118 | 464 |
| 2. Prohibitive | "Don't Ever" | Mt.6:34; Jn.3:7 | 118 | 469 |
| 3. Deliberative | Non-factual Question | Mk.12:14; Lk.3:10 | 119 | 465 |
| 4. Emphatic Negation | "Never" (ου μη) | Mt.5:20; Lk.6:37 | 119 | 468 |
| 5. Potential | Subordinate Clauses (various) | Jn.1:7; Rom.7:2 | 120 | 469 |

### C.  OPTATIVE  (Possibility)

| | | | | |
|---|---|---|---|---|
| 1. Voluntative | Wish, Prayer | Ac.8:20; 1 Pet.1:2 | 124 | 481 |
| 2. Potential | Futuristic; 4$^{th}$ class apodosis | Lk.1:62; Ac.8:31 | 125 | 483 |
| 3. Deliberative (Oblique) | Indirect Question | Lk.1:29; 22:23 | 125 | 483 |
| 4. Conditional | 4$^{th}$ class | 1 Pet.3:14; 3:17 | 126 | 484 |

### D.  IMPERATIVE  (Command)

| | | | | |
|---|---|---|---|---|
| 1. Command | Positive Demand | Mt.5:44; 6:6 | 127 | 485 |
| 2. Prohibition | "Stop" | 1 Cor.6:9; Rom. 6:12 | 127 | 487 |
| 3. Entreaty | Request ("Please") | Mk.9:22; Mt.6:13 | 128 | 487 |
| 4. Permission | Consent Given | Mt.8:32; 23:32 | 128 | 488 |
| 5. Condition? | Implied | Jn.2:19; Jas.4:7-8 | 129 | 492 |
| 6. Concession? | Implied | Eph.4:26; Jn.7:52 | 129 | -- |

# ASSIGNMENT

## IDENTIFY SYNTACTICAL FORMS/FUNCTIONS

## VOICE

## HEBREWS 2:5-16

A.  Identify the voice and its function
1. ὑπέταξεν (v. 5)

2. διεμαρτύρατο (v. 6)

3. μιμνῄσκῃ

4. ἐπισκέπτῃ

5. ἠλάττωσας (v. 7)

6. ὑποτεταγμένα (v. 8)

7. ἠλαττωμένον (v. 9)

8. γεύσηται

9. ἁγιάζων (v. 11)

10. ἁγιαζόμενοι

11. ἐπαισχύνεται

12. ἔσομαι (v. 13)

13. μετέσχεν (v. 14)

14. ἐπιλαμβάνεται (v. 16)

B.  Identify the case and its function
1. ἀγγέλοις (v. 5)

2. αὐτοῦ (v. 6)

3. ἀνθρώπου

4. δόξῃ (v. 7)

5. αὐτῷ  (2nd; v. 8)

6. θανάτου (v. 9)

7. χάριτι

8. θανάτου

9. ἀρχηγὸν (v. 10)

10. σωτηρίας

11. ἀδελφοὺς (v. 11)

12. αἵματος (v. 14)

13. φόβῳ (v. 15)

14. δουλείας

15.  σπέρματος (v. 16)

C.  Identify the function of the article
1. τὴν (v. 5)
2. τῷ (v. 8)

3. τὰ
4. τὸν (v. 9)

# ASSIGNMENT

## IDENTIFY SYNTACTICAL FORMS/FUNCTIONS

## VOICE; MOOD

## JOHN 9:24-34, 40-41

A. Identify the voice and its function
   1. Ἐφώνησαν (v. 24)
   2. ἀπεκρίθη (v. 25)
   3. θέλετε (v. 27)

   4. ἠκούσθη (v. 32)
   5. ἠδύνατο (v. 33)
   6. ἐγεννήθης (v. 34)

B. Identify the mood and its function
   1. Ἐφώνησαν (v. 24)
   2. δὸς
   3. βλέπω (v. 25)
   4. ἐστιν
   5. ἐποίησέν (v. 26)

   6. εἶπεν (v. 30)
   7. ἀκούει (v. 31)
   8. ᾖ
   9. ποιῇ
   10. ἦν (v. 33)

C. Identify the function of the article
   1. τὸν (v. 24)
   2. τοὺς (v. 26)

   3. οἱ (v. 40)
   4. ἡ (v. 41)

D. Identify the case and its function
   1. δευτέρου (v. 24)
   2. ἁμαρτωλός
   3. τί (v. 27)
   4. μαθηταὶ
   5. Μωϋσέως (v. 28)

   6. Μωϋσεῖ (v. 29)
   7. ἁμαρτωλῶν (v. 31)
   8. ἁμαρτίαις (v. 34)
   9. ταῦτα (v. 40)
   10. τυφλοὶ (v.41)

# LESSON TEN:
# SYMBOLISM ABOUT HOLY SPIRIT/SPIRITUAL GIFTS

## Candlestick (Seven-Branched)

The seven-branched candlestick, often called a "menorah," is used by Christians to represent the Holy Spirit and its seven gifts: wisdom, understanding, counsel, might, knowledge, fear of the Lord, and delight in the Lord.

# LESSON TEN

## READING ABOUT HOLY SPIRIT/SPIRITUAL GIFTS

**John 16:12** Ἔτι πολλὰ ἔχω ὑμῖν λέγειν, ἀλλ' οὐ δύνασθε βαστάζειν ἄρτι· **13** ὅταν δὲ

ἔλθῃ ἐκεῖνος, τὸ πνεῦμα τῆς ἀληθείας, ὁδηγήσει ὑμᾶς ἐν τῇ ἀληθείᾳ πάσῃ· οὐ γὰρ

λαλήσει ἀφ' ἑαυτοῦ, ἀλλ' ὅσα ἀκούσει λαλήσει καὶ τὰ ἐρχόμενα ἀναγγελεῖ ὑμῖν. **14**

ἐκεῖνος ἐμὲ δοξάσει, ὅτι ἐκ τοῦ ἐμοῦ λήμψεται καὶ ἀναγγελεῖ ὑμῖν. **15** πάντα ὅσα ἔχει

ὁ πατὴρ ἐμά ἐστιν· διὰ τοῦτο εἶπον ὅτι ἐκ τοῦ ἐμοῦ λαμβάνει καὶ ἀναγγελεῖ ὑμῖν. **16**

Μικρὸν καὶ οὐκέτι θεωρεῖτέ με, καὶ πάλιν μικρὸν καὶ ὄψεσθέ με. **17** εἶπαν οὖν ἐκ

τῶν μαθητῶν αὐτοῦ πρὸς ἀλλήλους· τί ἐστιν τοῦτο ὃ λέγει ἡμῖν· μικρὸν καὶ οὐ

θεωρεῖτέ με, καὶ πάλιν μικρὸν καὶ ὄψεσθέ με; καί· ὅτι ὑπάγω πρὸς τὸν πατέρα; **18**

ἔλεγον οὖν· τί ἐστιν τοῦτο [ὃ λέγει] τὸ μικρόν; οὐκ οἴδαμεν τί λαλεῖ. **19** Ἔγνω [ὁ]

Ἰησοῦς ὅτι ἤθελον αὐτὸν ἐρωτᾶν, καὶ εἶπεν αὐτοῖς· περὶ τούτου ζητεῖτε μετ' ἀλλήλων

ὅτι εἶπον· μικρὸν καὶ οὐ θεωρεῖτέ με, καὶ πάλιν μικρὸν καὶ ὄψεσθέ με; **20** ἀμὴν ἀμὴν

λέγω ὑμῖν ὅτι κλαύσετε καὶ θρηνήσετε ὑμεῖς, ὁ δὲ κόσμος χαρήσεται· ὑμεῖς

λυπηθήσεσθε, ἀλλ' ἡ λύπη ὑμῶν εἰς χαρὰν γενήσεται. **21** ἡ γυνὴ ὅταν τίκτῃ λύπην ἔχει, ὅτι ἦλθεν ἡ ὥρα αὐτῆς· ὅταν δὲ γεννήσῃ τὸ παιδίον, οὐκέτι μνημονεύει τῆς

θλίψεως διὰ τὴν χαρὰν ὅτι ἐγεννήθη ἄνθρωπος εἰς τὸν κόσμον. **22** καὶ ὑμεῖς οὖν νῦν

μὲν λύπην ἔχετε· πάλιν δὲ ὄψομαι ὑμᾶς, καὶ χαρήσεται ὑμῶν ἡ καρδία, καὶ τὴν χαρὰν

ὑμῶν οὐδεὶς αἴρει ἀφ' ὑμῶν. **23** Καὶ ἐν ἐκείνῃ τῇ ἡμέρᾳ ἐμὲ οὐκ ἐρωτήσετε οὐδέν.

ἀμὴν ἀμὴν λέγω ὑμῖν, ἄν τι αἰτήσητε τὸν πατέρα ἐν τῷ ὀνόματί μου δώσει ὑμῖν. **24**

ἕως ἄρτι οὐκ ᾐτήσατε οὐδὲν ἐν τῷ ὀνόματί μου· αἰτεῖτε καὶ λήμψεσθε, ἵνα ἡ χαρὰ

ὑμῶν ᾖ πεπληρωμένη.


**Ephesians 4:7** Ἑνὶ δὲ ἑκάστῳ ἡμῶν ἐδόθη ἡ χάρις κατὰ τὸ μέτρον τῆς δωρεᾶς τοῦ

Χριστοῦ. **8** διὸ λέγει· ἀναβὰς εἰς ὕψος ᾐχμαλώτευσεν αἰχμαλωσίαν, ἔδωκεν δόματα

τοῖς ἀνθρώποις. **9** τὸ δὲ ἀνέβη τί ἐστιν, εἰ μὴ ὅτι καὶ κατέβη εἰς τὰ κατώτερα [μέρη]

τῆς γῆς; **10** ὁ καταβὰς αὐτός ἐστιν καὶ ὁ ἀναβὰς ὑπεράνω πάντων τῶν οὐρανῶν, ἵνα

πληρώσῃ τὰ πάντα. **11** Καὶ αὐτὸς ἔδωκεν τοὺς μὲν ἀποστόλους, τοὺς δὲ προφήτας, τοὺς

δὲ εὐαγγελιστάς, τοὺς δὲ ποιμένας καὶ διδασκάλους, **12** πρὸς τὸν καταρτισμὸν τῶν

ἁγίων εἰς ἔργον διακονίας, εἰς οἰκοδομὴν τοῦ σώματος τοῦ Χριστοῦ, **13** μέχρι καταντήσωμεν οἱ πάντες εἰς τὴν ἑνότητα τῆς πίστεως καὶ τῆς ἐπιγνώσεως τοῦ υἱοῦ τοῦ

θεοῦ, εἰς ἄνδρα τέλειον, εἰς μέτρον ἡλικίας τοῦ πληρώματος τοῦ Χριστοῦ, 14 ἵνα

μηκέτι ὦμεν νήπιοι, κλυδωνιζόμενοι καὶ περιφερόμενοι παντὶ ἀνέμῳ τῆς διδασκαλίας

ἐν τῇ κυβείᾳ τῶν ἀνθρώπων, ἐν πανουργίᾳ πρὸς τὴν μεθοδείαν τῆς πλάνης, 15

ἀληθεύοντες δὲ ἐν ἀγάπῃ αὐξήσωμεν εἰς αὐτὸν τὰ πάντα, ὅς ἐστιν ἡ κεφαλή, Χριστός,

16 ἐξ οὗ πᾶν τὸ σῶμα συναρμολογούμενον καὶ συμβιβαζόμενον διὰ πάσης ἁφῆς τῆς

ἐπιχορηγίας κατ᾽ ἐνέργειαν ἐν μέτρῳ ἑνὸς ἑκάστου μέρους τὴν αὔξησιν τοῦ σώματος

ποιεῖται εἰς οἰκοδομὴν ἑαυτοῦ ἐν ἀγάπῃ.


**1 Corinthians 12:1** Περὶ δὲ τῶν πνευματικῶν, ἀδελφοί, οὐ θέλω ὑμᾶς ἀγνοεῖν. 2

Οἴδατε ὅτι ὅτε ἔθνη ἦτε πρὸς τὰ εἴδωλα τὰ ἄφωνα ὡς ἂν ἤγεσθε ἀπαγόμενοι. 3 διὸ

γνωρίζω ὑμῖν ὅτι οὐδεὶς ἐν πνεύματι θεοῦ λαλῶν λέγει, Ἀνάθεμα Ἰησοῦς, καὶ οὐδεὶς

δύναται εἰπεῖν, Κύριος Ἰησοῦς, εἰ μὴ ἐν πνεύματι ἁγίῳ. 4 Διαιρέσεις δὲ χαρισμάτων

εἰσίν, τὸ δὲ αὐτὸ πνεῦμα· 5 καὶ διαιρέσεις διακονιῶν εἰσιν, καὶ ὁ αὐτὸς κύριος· 6

καὶ διαιρέσεις ἐνεργημάτων εἰσίν, ὁ δὲ αὐτὸς θεὸς ὁ ἐνεργῶν τὰ πάντα ἐν πᾶσιν. 7

ἑκάστῳ δὲ δίδοται ἡ φανέρωσις τοῦ πνεύματος πρὸς τὸ συμφέρον. 8 ᾧ μὲν γὰρ διὰ τοῦ

πνεύματος δίδοται λόγος σοφίας, ἄλλῳ δὲ λόγος γνώσεως κατὰ τὸ αὐτὸ πνεῦμα, 9

ἑτέρῳ πίστις ἐν τῷ αὐτῷ πνεύματι, ἄλλῳ δὲ χαρίσματα ἰαμάτων ἐν τῷ ἑνὶ πνεύματι,

10 ἄλλῳ δὲ ἐνεργήματα δυνάμεων, ἄλλῳ [δὲ] προφητεία, ἄλλῳ [δὲ] διακρίσεις

πνευμάτων, ἑτέρῳ γένη γλωσσῶν, ἄλλῳ δὲ ἑρμηνεία γλωσσῶν· 11 πάντα δὲ ταῦτα

ἐνεργεῖ τὸ ἓν καὶ τὸ αὐτὸ πνεῦμα διαιροῦν ἰδίᾳ ἑκάστῳ καθὼς βούλεται.

## QUESTIONS FOR HEART AND MIND

### HOLY SPIRIT/SPIRITUAL GIFTS

### EPHESIANS 4:7-16

1. What is the textual problem involving the quote of Psalm 68:18?

2. What proof for the descent of Christ to Hades appears in verse 9? How does syntax affect this idea?

3. What use of the article affects the number of the gifts of verse 11 and what are the options?

4. List five characteristics (descriptions) of the Church.

5. Give three traits of immaturity/imperfection.

6. How is the Church, the body of Christ, more mature today than in the past? How can we contribute to it to make it more so?

# QUESTIONS FOR HEART AND MIND

## HOLY SPIRIT/SPIRITUAL GIFTS

### 1 CORINTHIANS 12:1-11

1. How is the deity of the Holy Spirit implicit (v. 3)?

2. What different ideas do the prepositions of verses 8-9 present as used with the Holy Spirit?

3. Give three traits of the giving of the gifts by the Spirit.

# CLASS DISCUSSION QUESTIONS

## TENSE : PRESENT

## HOLY SPIRIT/SPIRITUAL GIFTS

## EPHESIANS 4:7-16

1.   What are the possibilities for the present λέγει (4:8)?

How does this affect our view of Scripture?

2.   What are the possibilities for ἐστιν in 4:10?

3.   What are the possibilities for ἐστιν in 4:15?

4.   What are the implications for our doctrine of the church and the role of women in ministry and in the home (cf. 1 Cor. 11; Eph. 5)?

# CLASS DISCUSSION QUESTIONS

## TENSES:  PRESENT, IMPERFECT

## HOLY SPIRIT/SPIRITUAL GIFTS

## 1 CORINTHIANS 12:1-11

1. Why is it appropriate for Paul to use the imperfect tenses in verse 2?

2. Why is the supplying of the missing present tense of the copula (ἐστιν) appropriate in verse 3?

3. How many times does the present tense occur in verses 4-11?

   Considering that the present tense should also be understood many more times, how may we account for this frequency?

   What use of the present tense explains this phenomenon?

4. What does the predominance of this particular use of the present suggest regarding the existence of all the spiritual gifts, including the "sign gifts"?

   Is this passage descriptive or normative?

# TENSE (Aspect, Aktionsart)

| Function | Key Concepts | N.T. Example | B&W | Wall |
|---|---|---|---|---|
| **PRESENT  (Linear)** | | | | |
| 1. Descriptive | Pictorial | Mt.8:25; Jn.5:7 | 84 | 518 |
| linear    2. Durative | Progressive (adv.) | Lk.13:7; Jn.15:27 | 84 | 519 |
| action    3. Iterative | Repeated Action | Rom.8:36; 1 Cor.15:31 | 85 | 520-1 |
| (cf. Customary) | | | | |
| 4. Tendential | Proposed, attempted | Gal.5:4; Jn.10:32 | 86 | 534 |
| (conative) | "try, attempt" | | | |
| 5. Gnomic | Universal Truth | Mt. 7:17; 2 Cor.9:7 | 86 | 523 |
| punctiliar  6. Historical (Dram.) | Past as Present | Mt.3:1; Jn.1:29 | 87 | 526 |
| (unlimited)7. Futuristic | Fut. as Present | Jn.14:3; Mt.27:63 | 88 | 535 |
| action    8. Aoristic | Punctiliar | Mk.2:5; Ac.16:18 | 89 | 517 |
| perfective 9. Perfective | Existing Results | Lk.15:27; Gal.1:6 | 89 | 532 |
| action | | | | |
| **IMPERFECT (Linear Past)** | | | | |
| 1. Descriptive | Pictorial | Gal.1:13; Mk.12:41 | 91 | 543 |
| 2. Durative | Progressive | Lk.2:49; 1 Cor. 3:6 | 91 | -- |
| 3. Iterative | "Kept on, Used to" | Mk.15:6; Ac.3:2 | 93 | 546-8 |
| (cf. Customary) | | | | |
| 4. Tendential | "We're going to, | Mt.3:14; Lk.1:59 | 93 | 550 |
| (conative) | trying to" | | | |
| 5. Voluntative | Potential; A wish | Rom.9:3; Gal.4:20 | 94 | 550 |
| 6. Inceptive | "Began" | Mk.5:32; Ac.3:8 | 95 | 544 |
| (inchoative) | | | | |

# ASSIGNMENT

## IDENTIFY SYNTACTICAL FORMS/FUNCTIONS:  TENSE

## PRESENT

## EPHESIANS 4:7-16

A. Identify the function of the present
   1. λέγει  (v. 8)

   2. ἐστιν (v. 9)

   3. ἐστιν (v. 10)

   4. ὦμεν (v. 14)

   5. ἀληθεύοντες (v. 15)

   6. ἐστιν

   7. ποιεῖται  (v. 16)

B. Identify the case and its function
   1. Ἑνὶ (v. 7)

   2. δωρεᾶς

   3. αἰχμαλωσίαν  (v. 8)

   4. δόματα

   5. γῆς (v. 9)

   6. ἀγίων (v. 12)

   7. διακονίας

   8. σώματος

   9. πίστεως (v. 13)

   10. ἐπιγνώσεως

   11. υἱοῦ

   12. πληρώματος

   13. ἀνέμω (v. 14)

   14. διδασκαλίας

   15. ἀνθρώπων

   16. πλάνης

   17. Χριστός  (v. 15)

   18. ἐπιχορηγίας  (v. 16)

C. Identify the use of the article
   1. τῆς (v. 7)

   2. τοῖς (v. 8)

   3. τὸ (v. 9)

   4. ὁ (v. 10)

   5. τοὺς (v. 11)

   6. τὸ (v. 16)

# ASSIGNMENT

## IDENTIFY SYNTACTICAL FORMS/FUNCTIONS:  TENSES

## PRESENT, IMPERFECT

## 1 CORINTHIANS 12:1-11

A.  Identify the tense and its function

    1. ἦτε (v. 2)              5. εἰσίν (v. 4)

    2. ἤγεσθε                 6. δίδοται (v. 7)

    3. γνωρίζω (v. 3)        7. ἐνεργεῖ (v.11)

    4. λέγει                  8. βούλεται

B.  Identify the case and its function

    1. ἀδελφοί (v. 1)       6. πνεύματος (v. 7)

    2. ἔθνη (v. 2)          7. σοφίας (v. 8)

    3. ὑμῖν (v. 3)          8. ἰαμάτων (v. 9)

    4. ᾿Ανάθεμα         9. ταῦτα (v. 11)

    5. χαρισμάτων (v. 4)    10. πνεῦμα

C.  Identify the use of the article

    1. τῶν (v. 1)          4. τοῦ (v. 7)

    2. τὰ (v. 2)           5. τὸ

    3. τὸ (v. 4)          6. τὸ (1st; v. 11)

# LESSON ELEVEN:
## SYMBOLISM ABOUT THE CHURCH/SIN

## Ship

The ship symbolizes the church, and the refuge therein. Noah's ark was a place of safety. Jesus calmed the storm, and those in the boat with Him were safe. The central area in a church from narthex to chancel is usually called the "nave", which is the Latin word for "ship".

## The Gospel Mill

A hand-mill is pictured, with prophets, law-givers, evangelists and apostles emptying grain into the mill. The Church is turning the mill, and the Lord stands by with His right hand raised in blessing. It is intended to represent the precious seeds of Old Testament prophecy and New Testament truth converted into flour which is transformed into the Bread of Life.(Taken from F.R.Webber, *Church Symbolism,* GaleResearch Center, Detroit,

# LESSON ELEVEN

## READING ABOUT THE CHURCH/SIN

**John 16:25** Ταῦτα ἐν παροιμίαις λελάληκα ὑμῖν· ἔρχεται ὥρα ὅτε οὐκέτι ἐν

παροιμίαις λαλήσω ὑμῖν, ἀλλὰ παρρησίᾳ περὶ τοῦ πατρὸς ἀπαγγελῶ ὑμῖν. **26** ἐν

ἐκείνῃ τῇ ἡμέρᾳ ἐν τῷ ὀνόματί μου αἰτήσεσθε, καὶ οὐ λέγω ὑμῖν ὅτι ἐγὼ ἐρωτήσω τὸν

πατέρα περὶ ὑμῶν· **27** αὐτὸς γὰρ ὁ πατὴρ φιλεῖ ὑμᾶς, ὅτι ὑμεῖς ἐμὲ πεφιλήκατε καὶ

πεπιστεύκατε ὅτι ἐγὼ παρὰ [τοῦ] θεοῦ ἐξῆλθον. **28** ἐξῆλθον παρὰ τοῦ πατρὸς καὶ

ἐλήλυθα εἰς τὸν κόσμον· πάλιν ἀφίημι τὸν κόσμον καὶ πορεύομαι πρὸς τὸν πατέρα. **29**

Λέγουσιν οἱ μαθηταὶ αὐτοῦ· ἴδε νῦν ἐν παρρησίᾳ λαλεῖς καὶ παροιμίαν οὐδεμίαν

λέγεις. **30** νῦν οἴδαμεν ὅτι οἶδας πάντα καὶ οὐ χρείαν ἔχεις ἵνα τίς σε ἐρωτᾷ· ἐν

τούτῳ πιστεύομεν ὅτι ἀπὸ θεοῦ ἐξῆλθες. **31** ἀπεκρίθη αὐτοῖς Ἰησοῦς· ἄρτι πιστεύετε;

**32** ἰδοὺ ἔρχεται ὥρα καὶ ἐλήλυθεν ἵνα σκορπισθῆτε ἕκαστος εἰς τὰ ἴδια κἀμὲ μόνον

ἀφῆτε· καὶ οὐκ εἰμὶ μόνος, ὅτι ὁ πατὴρ μετ᾽ ἐμοῦ ἐστιν. **33** ταῦτα λελάληκα ὑμῖν ἵνα

ἐν ἐμοὶ εἰρήνην ἔχητε. ἐν τῷ κόσμῳ θλῖψιν ἔχετε· ἀλλὰ θαρσεῖτε, ἐγὼ νενίκηκα τὸν

κόσμον.

**1 Timothy 2:5** εἷς γὰρ θεός, εἷς καὶ μεσίτης θεοῦ καὶ ἀνθρώπων, ἄνθρωπος Χριστὸς

Ἰησοῦς, **6** ὁ δοὺς ἑαυτὸν ἀντίλυτρον ὑπὲρ πάντων, τὸ μαρτύριον καιροῖς ἰδίοις. **7** εἰς

ὃ ἐτέθην ἐγὼ κῆρυξ καὶ ἀπόστολος, ἀλήθειαν λέγω οὐ ψεύδομαι, διδάσκαλος ἐθνῶν ἐν

πίστει καὶ ἀληθείᾳ. **8** Βούλομαι οὖν προσεύχεσθαι τοὺς ἄνδρας ἐν παντὶ τόπῳ

ἐπαίροντας ὁσίους χεῖρας χωρὶς ὀργῆς καὶ διαλογισμοῦ. **9** Ὡσαύτως [καὶ] γυναῖκας ἐν

καταστολῇ κοσμίῳ μετὰ αἰδοῦς καὶ σωφροσύνης κοσμεῖν ἑαυτάς, μὴ ἐν πλέγμασιν καὶ

χρυσίῳ ἢ μαργαρίταις ἢ ἱματισμῷ πολυτελεῖ, **10** ἀλλ’ ὃ πρέπει γυναιξὶν

ἐπαγγελλομέναις θεοσέβειαν, δι’ ἔργων ἀγαθῶν. **11** Γυνὴ ἐν ἡσυχίᾳ μανθανέτω ἐν πάσῃ

ὑποταγῇ· **12** διδάσκειν δὲ γυναικὶ οὐκ ἐπιτρέπω οὐδὲ αὐθεντεῖν ἀνδρός, ἀλλ’ εἶναι ἐν

ἡσυχίᾳ. **13** Ἀδὰμ γὰρ πρῶτος ἐπλάσθη, εἶτα Εὕα. **14** καὶ Ἀδὰμ οὐκ ἠπατήθη, ἡ δὲ

γυνὴ ἐξαπατηθεῖσα ἐν παραβάσει γέγονεν· **15** σωθήσεται δὲ διὰ τῆς τεκνογονίας, ἐὰν

μείνωσιν ἐν πίστει καὶ ἀγάπῃ καὶ ἁγιασμῷ μετὰ σωφροσύνης·

**Romans 5:12** Διὰ τοῦτο ὥσπερ δι' ἑνὸς ἀνθρώπου ἡ ἁμαρτία εἰς τὸν κόσμον εἰσῆλθεν

καὶ διὰ τῆς ἁμαρτίας ὁ θάνατος, καὶ οὕτως εἰς πάντας ἀνθρώπους ὁ θάνατος διῆλθεν,

ἐφ' ᾧ πάντες ἥμαρτον· **13** ἄχρι γὰρ νόμου ἁμαρτία ἦν ἐν κόσμῳ, ἁμαρτία δὲ οὐκ

ἐλλογεῖται μὴ ὄντος νόμου, **14** ἀλλὰ ἐβασίλευσεν ὁ θάνατος ἀπὸ Ἀδὰμ μέχρι Μωϋσέως

καὶ ἐπὶ τοὺς μὴ ἁμαρτήσαντας ἐπὶ τῷ ὁμοιώματι τῆς παραβάσεως Ἀδὰμ ὅς ἐστιν τύπος

τοῦ μέλλοντος. **15** Ἀλλ' οὐχ ὡς τὸ παράπτωμα, οὕτως καὶ τὸ χάρισμα· εἰ γὰρ τῷ τοῦ

ἑνὸς παραπτώματι οἱ πολλοὶ ἀπέθανον, πολλῷ μᾶλλον ἡ χάρις τοῦ θεοῦ καὶ ἡ δωρεὰ ἐν

χάριτι τῇ τοῦ ἑνὸς ἀνθρώπου Ἰησοῦ Χριστοῦ εἰς τοὺς πολλοὺς ἐπερίσσευσεν. **16** καὶ

οὐχ ὡς δι' ἑνὸς ἁμαρτήσαντος τὸ δώρημα· τὸ μὲν γὰρ κρίμα ἐξ ἑνὸς εἰς κατάκριμα, τὸ

δὲ χάρισμα ἐκ πολλῶν παραπτωμάτων εἰς δικαίωμα. **17** εἰ γὰρ τῷ τοῦ ἑνὸς

παραπτώματι ὁ θάνατος ἐβασίλευσεν διὰ τοῦ ἑνός, πολλῷ μᾶλλον οἱ τὴν περισσείαν τῆς

χάριτος καὶ τῆς δωρεᾶς τῆς δικαιοσύνης λαμβάνοντες ἐν ζωῇ βασιλεύσουσιν διὰ τοῦ

ἑνὸς Ἰησοῦ Χριστοῦ. **18** Ἄρα οὖν ὡς δι' ἑνὸς παραπτώματος εἰς πάντας ἀνθρώπους

εἰς κατάκριμα, οὕτως καὶ δι' ἑνὸς δικαιώματος εἰς πάντας ἀνθρώπους εἰς δικαίωσιν

ζωῆς· **19** ὥσπερ γὰρ διὰ τῆς παρακοῆς τοῦ ἑνὸς ἀνθρώπου ἁμαρτωλοὶ κατεστάθησαν οἱ πολλοί, οὕτως καὶ διὰ τῆς ὑπακοῆς τοῦ ἑνὸς δίκαιοι κατασταθήσονται οἱ πολλοί. 20

νόμος δὲ παρεισῆλθεν, ἵνα πλεονάσῃ τὸ παράπτωμα· οὗ δὲ ἐπλεόνασεν ἡ ἁμαρτία,

ὑπερεπερίσσευσεν ἡ χάρις, 21 ἵνα ὥσπερ ἐβασίλευσεν ἡ ἁμαρτία ἐν τῷ θανάτῳ, οὕτως

καὶ ἡ χάρις βασιλεύσῃ διὰ δικαιοσύνης εἰς ζωὴν αἰώνιον διὰ Ἰησοῦ Χριστοῦ τοῦ

κυρίου ἡμῶν.

# QUESTIONS FOR HEART AND MIND

## THE CHURCH/SIN

### 1 TIMOTHY 2:5-15

1. Give four characteristics of Christ in verses 5-6.

2. How does verse 6 impact the extent of the atonement?

3. In what three ways does Paul view himself in connection to the witness?

4. How do verses 8-15 impact church functions by men and women?

5. What subtle shift occurs between verses 10-11?

6. How are verses 13-14 significant for church life?

# QUESTIONS FOR HEART AND MIND

## THE CHURCH/SIN

## ROMANS 5:12-21

1. How are people reckoned as sinners (vv. 12-14)?

2. Construct in parallel the clauses of verse 17. Why are there differences?

3. How does the passage stress that grace exceeds judgment?

4. How can it be "fair" for God to judge us for what Adam did?

# TENSE

**FUTURE (Punctiliar)**

| | | | | |
|---|---|---|---|---|
| 1. Predictive | Future event, state | Ac.2:19; Jn.14:26 | 95 | 568 |
| 2. Progressive | "Keep on" | Rom.6:2; Phil.1:18 | 96 | -- |
| 3. Imperative | "You shall" (cohort) | Mt.1:21; 5:21 | 97 | 569 |
| 4. Deliberative | Rhetorical or real question | Rom.3:6; Mt.11:16 Rom.6:2 | 97 | 570 |
| 5. Gnomic | Universal (few) | Gal.6:5; Rom.5:7 | 98 | 571 |

**AORIST (Punctiliar)**

| | | | | |
|---|---|---|---|---|
| 1. Constative | Action in entirety | Mt.8:3; Heb.11:13 | 99 | 557 |
| 2. Ingressive | Entrance into state or condition | Ac.15:12; Jn.1:14 | 99 | 558 |
| 3. Culminative | Results, completion of action | Lk.1:1, Ac.5:4 | 100 | 559 |
| 4. Gnomic | Universal | Lk.7:35; Jas.1:11 | 101 | 562 |
| 5. Epistolary | Future as fact (reader's perspective) | Ac.23:30; Col.4:8 | 102 | 562 |
| 6. Dramatic | Present as past | Mt.3:17; 9:18 | 102 | 564 |
| 7. Proleptic | Future as fact | Jn.15:8; Gal.5:4 | 103 | 563 |

# CLASS DISCUSSION QUESTIONS

## TENSES:  FUTURE; AORIST

## THE CHURCH/SIN

## 1 TIMOTHY 2:5-15

1.  What tense is the participle δούς (v. 6)?


    What is significant about this tense form in light of the general lack of verb
    forms in the surrounding verses (vv. 5-7)?  Why are verb forms absent?


2.  What observations might we make regarding the prevalent use of the present tense in
    verses 8-12?


    What function of the present is probable?


3.  What is significant about Paul's use of the aorist tense in verses 13-14?  What use of
    the aorist is this?


4.  What verb tense is emphasized (in v. 14) because of its only occurrence in this
    passage?


5.  What options exist for the function of the future σωθήσεται (v. 15)?


    How do these options affect the interpretation of the passage?


    Why is there only one future form in this passage?

# CLASS DISCUSSION QUESTIONS

## TENSES:  FUTURE, AORIST

### CHURCH/SIN

### ROMANS 5:12-21

1.      What are the possible functions of the aorist ἥμαρτον (5:12)?

         What are the implications of each?

2.      What are the possible functions of the aorist ἐβασίλευσεν (5:14)?

         What are the implications of each?

## ASSIGNMENT

### IDENTIFY SYNTACTICAL FUNCTIONS:  TENSES

### PRESENT, IMPERFECT, FUTURE

### 1 TIMOTHY 2:5-15

A. Identify the tense and its function

1. λέγω (v. 7)

2. ψεύδομαι

3. Βούλομαι (v. 8)

4. πρέπει (v. 10)

5. μανθανέτω (v. 11)

6. ἐπιτρέπω (v. 12)

7. σωθήσεται  (v. 15)

B. Identify the case and its function

1. εἷς (1st) (v. 5)

2. θεός

3. θεοῦ

4. ἄνθρωπος

5. ἑαυτὸν (v. 6)

6. ἀντίλυτρον

7. μαρτύριον

8. καιροῖς

9. κῆρυξ (v. 7)

10. ἐθνῶν

11. ἄνδρας (v. 8)

12. γυναῖκας (v. 9)

13. ἑαυτάς

14. χρυσίῳ

15. γυναικὶ (v. 12)

16. ἀνδρός

17. Εὕα (v. 13)

18. ἀγάπη (v. 15)

# ASSIGNMENT

## IDENTIFY SYNTACTICAL FUNCTIONS: TENSES

## PRESENT, IMPERFECT, FUTURE, AORIST

## ROMANS 5:12-21

A.  Identify the tense and its function

1. εἰσῆλθεν (v. 12)

8. ἀπέθανον (v. 15)

2. διῆλθεν

9. ἐβασίλευσεν (v. 17)

3. ἥμαρτον

10. βασιλεύσουσιν

4. ἦν (v. 13)

11. κατεστάθησαν (v. 19)

5. ἐλλογεῖται

12. κατασταθήσονται

6. ἐβασίλευσεν (v. 14)

13. ἐπλεόνασεν (v. 20)

7. ἐστιν

14. βασιλεύσῃ (v. 21)

B.  Identify the case and its function

1. θάνατος (v. 12)

8. χάριτος (v. 17)

2. νόμου (2ⁿᵈ) (v. 13)

9. δικαιοσύνης

3. Ἀδὰμ (2ⁿᵈ) (v. 14)

10. ζωῆς (v. 18)

4. παραπτώματι (v. 15)

11. ἁμαρτωλοὶ (v. 19)

5. ἑνὸς

12. παράπτωμα (v. 20)

6. θεοῦ

13. κυρίου (v. 21)

7. Ἰησοῦ

# LESSON TWELVE:
## SYMBOLISM ABOUT SALVATION

Pelican

The Pelican is symbolic of Jesus' atoning work on the cross for us (atoning meaning that His death and resurrection made us free from the penalty of our sins). Tradition says that the pelican, in times of famine, rips open it's own breast and feeds it's young her blood. The pelican dies so that her young may live. In the same way, Jesus died so that we may live.

# LESSON TWELVE

## READING ABOUT SALVATION

**John 17:1** Ταῦτα ἐλάλησεν Ἰησοῦς καὶ ἐπάρας τοὺς ὀφθαλμοὺς αὐτοῦ εἰς τὸν οὐρανὸν

εἶπεν· πάτερ, ἐλήλυθεν ἡ ὥρα· δόξασόν σου τὸν υἱόν, ἵνα ὁ υἱὸς δοξάσῃ σέ, **2** καθὼς

ἔδωκας αὐτῷ ἐξουσίαν πάσης σαρκός, ἵνα πᾶν ὃ δέδωκας αὐτῷ δώσῃ αὐτοῖς ζωὴν

αἰώνιον. **3** αὕτη δέ ἐστιν ἡ αἰώνιος ζωὴ ἵνα γινώσκωσιν σὲ τὸν μόνον ἀληθινὸν θεὸν

καὶ ὃν ἀπέστειλας Ἰησοῦν Χριστόν. **4** ἐγώ σε ἐδόξασα ἐπὶ τῆς γῆς τὸ ἔργον τελειώσας

ὃ δέδωκάς μοι ἵνα ποιήσω· **5** καὶ νῦν δόξασόν με σύ, πάτερ, παρὰ σεαυτῷ τῇ δόξῃ ᾗ

εἶχον πρὸ τοῦ τὸν κόσμον εἶναι παρὰ σοί.


**John 3:2** [2] οὗτος ἦλθεν πρὸς αὐτὸν νυκτὸς καὶ εἶπεν αὐτῷ· ῥαββί, οἴδαμεν ὅτι ἀπὸ

θεοῦ ἐλήλυθας διδάσκαλος· οὐδεὶς γὰρ δύναται ταῦτα τὰ σημεῖα ποιεῖν ἃ σὺ ποιεῖς, ἐὰν

μὴ ᾖ ὁ θεὸς μετ' αὐτοῦ. [3] ἀπεκρίθη Ἰησοῦς καὶ εἶπεν αὐτῷ· ἀμὴν ἀμὴν λέγω σοι, ἐὰν

μή τις γεννηθῇ ἄνωθεν, οὐ δύναται ἰδεῖν τὴν βασιλείαν τοῦ θεοῦ. [4] λέγει πρὸς αὐτὸν

[ὁ] Νικόδημος· πῶς δύναται ἄνθρωπος γεννηθῆναι γέρων ὤν; μὴ δύναται εἰς τὴν

κοιλίαν τῆς μητρὸς αὐτοῦ δεύτερον εἰσελθεῖν καὶ γεννηθῆναι; [5] ἀπεκρίθη Ἰησοῦς·

ἀμὴν ἀμὴν λέγω σοι, ἐὰν μή τις γεννηθῇ ἐξ ὕδατος καὶ πνεύματος, οὐ δύναται

εἰσελθεῖν εἰς τὴν βασιλείαν τοῦ θεοῦ. ⁶ τὸ γεγεννημένον ἐκ τῆς σαρκὸς σάρξ ἐστιν,

καὶ τὸ γεγεννημένον ἐκ τοῦ πνεύματος πνεῦμά ἐστιν. ⁷ μὴ θαυμάσῃς ὅτι εἶπόν σοι· δεῖ

ὑμᾶς γεννηθῆναι ἄνωθεν. ⁸ τὸ πνεῦμα ὅπου θέλει πνεῖ καὶ τὴν φωνὴν αὐτοῦ ἀκούεις,

ἀλλ᾽ οὐκ οἶδας πόθεν ἔρχεται καὶ ποῦ ὑπάγει· οὕτως ἐστὶν πᾶς ὁ γεγεννημένος ἐκ τοῦ

πνεύματος. ⁹ ἀπεκρίθη Νικόδημος καὶ εἶπεν αὐτῷ· πῶς δύναται ταῦτα γενέσθαι; ¹⁰

ἀπεκρίθη Ἰησοῦς καὶ εἶπεν αὐτῷ· σὺ εἶ ὁ διδάσκαλος τοῦ Ἰσραὴλ καὶ ταῦτα οὐ

γινώσκεις; ¹¹ ἀμὴν ἀμὴν λέγω σοι ὅτι ὃ οἴδαμεν λαλοῦμεν καὶ ὃ ἑωράκαμεν

μαρτυροῦμεν, καὶ τὴν μαρτυρίαν ἡμῶν οὐ λαμβάνετε. ¹² εἰ τὰ ἐπίγεια εἶπον ὑμῖν καὶ

οὐ πιστεύετε, πῶς ἐὰν εἴπω ὑμῖν τὰ ἐπουράνια πιστεύσετε; ¹³ καὶ οὐδεὶς ἀναβέβηκεν

εἰς τὸν οὐρανὸν εἰ μὴ ὁ ἐκ τοῦ οὐρανοῦ καταβάς, ὁ υἱὸς τοῦ ἀνθρώπου. ¹⁴ Καὶ καθὼς

Μωϋσῆς ὕψωσεν τὸν ὄφιν ἐν τῇ ἐρήμῳ, οὕτως ὑψωθῆναι δεῖ τὸν υἱὸν τοῦ ἀνθρώπου,

¹⁵ ἵνα πᾶς ὁ πιστεύων ἐν αὐτῷ ἔχῃ ζωὴν αἰώνιον. ¹⁶ οὕτως γὰρ ἠγάπησεν ὁ θεὸς τὸν

κόσμον, ὥστε τὸν υἱὸν τὸν μονογενῆ ἔδωκεν, ἵνα πᾶς ὁ πιστεύων εἰς αὐτὸν μὴ

ἀπόληται ἀλλ᾽ ἔχῃ ζωὴν αἰώνιον. ¹⁷ οὐ γὰρ ἀπέστειλεν ὁ θεὸς τὸν υἱὸν εἰς τὸν κόσμον ἵνα κρίνῃ τὸν κόσμον, ἀλλ' ἵνα σωθῇ ὁ κόσμος δι' αὐτοῦ. [18] ὁ πιστεύων εἰς

αὐτὸν οὐ κρίνεται· ὁ δὲ μὴ πιστεύων ἤδη κέκριται, ὅτι μὴ πεπίστευκεν εἰς τὸ ὄνομα

τοῦ μονογενοῦς υἱοῦ τοῦ θεοῦ. [19] αὕτη δέ ἐστιν ἡ κρίσις ὅτι τὸ φῶς ἐλήλυθεν εἰς τὸν

κόσμον καὶ ἠγάπησαν οἱ ἄνθρωποι μᾶλλον τὸ σκότος ἢ τὸ φῶς· ἦν γὰρ αὐτῶν πονηρὰ

τὰ ἔργα. [20] πᾶς γὰρ ὁ φαῦλα πράσσων μισεῖ τὸ φῶς καὶ οὐκ ἔρχεται πρὸς τὸ φῶς, ἵνα

μὴ ἐλεγχθῇ τὰ ἔργα αὐτοῦ· [21] ὁ δὲ ποιῶν τὴν ἀλήθειαν ἔρχεται πρὸς τὸ φῶς, ἵνα

φανερωθῇ αὐτοῦ τὰ ἔργα ὅτι ἐν θεῷ ἐστιν εἰργασμένα.

**Romans 3:21** Νυνὶ δὲ χωρὶς νόμου δικαιοσύνη θεοῦ πεφανέρωται μαρτυρουμένη ὑπὸ

τοῦ νόμου καὶ τῶν προφητῶν, **22** δικαιοσύνη δὲ θεοῦ διὰ πίστεως Ἰησοῦ Χριστοῦ εἰς

πάντας τοὺς πιστεύοντας. οὐ γάρ ἐστιν διαστολή, **23**    πάντες γὰρ ἥμαρτον καὶ

ὑστεροῦνται τῆς δόξης τοῦ θεοῦ **24**   δικαιούμενοι δωρεὰν τῇ αὐτοῦ χάριτι διὰ τῆς

ἀπολυτρώσεως τῆς ἐν Χριστῷ Ἰησοῦ· **25**   ὃν προέθετο ὁ θεὸς ἱλαστήριον διὰ [τῆς]

πίστεως ἐν τῷ αὐτοῦ αἵματι εἰς ἔνδειξιν τῆς δικαιοσύνης αὐτοῦ διὰ τὴν πάρεσιν τῶν

προγεγονότων ἁμαρτημάτων **26**   ἐν τῇ ἀνοχῇ τοῦ θεοῦ, πρὸς τὴν ἔνδειξιν τῆς

δικαιοσύνης αὐτοῦ ἐν τῷ νῦν καιρῷ, εἰς τὸ εἶναι αὐτὸν δίκαιον καὶ δικαιοῦντα τὸν ἐκ πίστεως Ἰησοῦ. **27** Ποῦ οὖν ἡ καύχησις; ἐξεκλείσθη. διὰ ποίου νόμου; τῶν ἔργων;

οὐχί, ἀλλὰ διὰ νόμου πίστεως. **28** λογιζόμεθα γὰρ δικαιοῦσθαι πίστει ἄνθρωπον χωρὶς

ἔργων νόμου. **29** ἢ Ἰουδαίων ὁ θεὸς μόνον; οὐχὶ καὶ ἐθνῶν; ναὶ καὶ ἐθνῶν, **30** εἴπερ

εἷς ὁ θεὸς ὃς δικαιώσει περιτομὴν ἐκ πίστεως καὶ ἀκροβυστίαν διὰ τῆς πίστεως. **31**

νόμον οὖν καταργοῦμεν διὰ τῆς πίστεως; μὴ γένοιτο· ἀλλὰ νόμον ἱστάνομεν.

# QUESTIONS FOR HEART AND MIND

## SALVATION

### JOHN 3:8-21

1. What was Nicodemus' problem?

2. How is the serpent parallel to Christ?

3. What is the significance of the perfect tenses in verse 18?

4. How does this passage contribute to soteriology?

5. What Old Testament allusions occur in verses 13-14?

# QUESTIONS FOR HEART AND MIND

## SALVATION

### ROMANS 3:21-31

1. List ten ways in which "righteousness by faith" is emphasized in the passage.

2. Write four observations about the grammar and terms of verse 23.

3. What is significant about the absence of the article with νόμου (3x) in verses 27-28?

4. What is significant about Paul's appeal to the "oneness" of God in verses 29-30?

5. Why does faith not abolish law (v. 31)?

# CLASS DISCUSSION QUESTIONS

## TENSES: PERFECT, PLUPERFECT

## SALVATION

## JOHN 3:8-21

1.      Identify the function of ἑωράκαμεν (3:11)?

     How does this term relate to the other perfect in the verse and help to function it?

     Is the reverse possible?

     What are the implications of the reverse?

2.      What are the possible functions of κέκριται (3:18)?

     What are the implications of these alternatives?

     What are the theological implications of each?

     Compare these results with the following πεπίστευκεν.

# CLASS DISCUSSION QUESTIONS

## TENSES:  PERFECT, PLUPERFECT

## SALVATION

## ROMANS 3:21-31

1.  What tense is πεφανέρωται and what are the possible functions of it (v. 21)?

    What are the implications for the possible functions?

    What use is the passive voice and what is the significance?

    How does the function of this verb relate to the following μαρτυρουμένη?

2.  Note the change in tenses of the verbs (ἥμαρτον and ὑστεροῦνται) in verse 23. What tenses are used and what are the possible functions?

    How does the change in tense help decide the function of each?

3.  What is the tense of προγεγονότων and what is the significance of this (v. 25)?

4.  What is the distinction, if any, between ἐκ and διὰ in verse 30?

5.  How might we explain the presence of so many present tenses in this passage? What function is involved?

# TENSE

## PERFECT (Complete)

| | | | | |
|---|---|---|---|---|
| 1. Intensive | Existing State (cf. Pres. Tense) | Lk.24:46; Jas.1:6 | 104 | 574 |
| 2. Consummative | Past, Completed Action | Ac.5:28; Rom.5:5 | 105 | 577 |
| 3. Iterative | Repeated (cf. Consum. Perfect) | Jn.1:18; 5:37 | 105 | -- |
| 4. Dramatic | Vivid Intensive Perfect | Jn.1:15; Rev.5:7 | 106 | 578 |
| 5. Gnomic ? | Universal | 1 Cor.7:39; Jn.3:18 | 107 | 580 |
| 6. Aoristic ? | No Result | Jn.12:29; 2 Cor.2:13 | 107 | 578 |

## PLUPERFECT (Past Perfect)

| | | | | |
|---|---|---|---|---|
| 1. Intensive | Abiding Results | Lk.4:41; Jn.18:16 | 108 | 584 |
| 2. Consummative | Completed Action | Lk.8:2; Ac.9:21 | 109 | 585 |

# ASSIGNMENT

## IDENTIFY SYNTACTICAL FORMS/FUNCTIONS:  TENSES

## PRESENT, IMPERFECT, FUTURE, AORIST, PERFECT, PLUPERFECT

## JOHN 3:8-21

A.  Identify the tense and its function

1. πνεῖ  (v. 8)                     10. ἀπέστειλεν (v. 17)

2. ἐστὶν                           11. κρίνεται  (v. 18)

3. ἑωράκαμεν (v. 11)                12. κέκριται

4. μαρτυροῦμεν                      13. πεπίστευκεν

5. πιστεύετε (v. 12)                14. ἐλήλυθεν (v. 19)

6. ἀναβέβηκεν (v. 13)               15. ἦν

7. ὕψωσεν (v. 14)                   16. μισεῖ  (v. 20)

8. ἔχῃ  (v. 15)                     17. ἔρχεται  (v. 21)

9. ἠγάπησεν (v. 16)

B.  Identify the case and its function
1. πνεῦμα (v. 8)                    8. υἱὸς (v. 13)

2. πνεύματος                        9. ἀνθρώπου

3. ταῦτα (v. 9)                     10. υἱὸν (v. 14)

4. αὐτῷ (v. 10)                     11. υἱοῦ (v. 18)

5. διδάσκαλος                       12. κρίσις (v. 19)

6. Ἰσραὴλ                           13. φῶς (1st)

7. ὃ (v. 11)

# ASSIGNMENT

## IDENTIFY SYNTACTICAL FORMS/FUNCTIONS: TENSES

## PRESENT, IMPERFECT, FUTURE, AORIST, PERFECT, PLUPERFECT

## ROMANS 3:21-31

A. Identify the tense and its function

1. πεφανέρωται (v. 21)
2. ἐστιν (v. 22)
3. ἥμαρτον (v. 23)
4. ὑστεροῦνται
5. προέθετο (v. 25)
6. ἐξεκλείσθη (v. 27)

7. λογιζόμεθα (v. 28)
8. δικαιώσει (v. 30)
9. καταργοῦμεν (v. 31)
10. γένοιτο
11. ἱστάνομεν

B. Identify the mood and its function

1. δικαιώσει (v. 30)

2. γένοιτο (v. 31)

C. Identify the voice and its function

1. πεφανέρωται (v. 21)
2. μαρτυρουμένη
3. ὑστεροῦνται (v. 23)
4. δικαιούμενοι (v. 24)

5. ἐξεκλείσθη (v. 27)
6. λογιζόμεθα (v. 28)
7. δικαιώσει (v. 30)

D. Identify the case and its function

1. θεοῦ (v. 21)
2. νόμου (2nd)
3. Ἰησοῦ (v. 22)
4. δόξης (v. 23)
5. δωρεὰν (v. 24)
6. χάριτι (v. 24)
7. ἱλαστήριον (v. 25)

8. δικαιοσύνης
9. θεοῦ (v. 26)
10. αὐτὸν
11. δίκαιον
12. ἔργων (v. 27)
13. πίστει (v. 28)
14. ἐθνῶν (v. 29)

# LESSON THIRTEEN:
## SYMBOLISM ABOUT THE ADVENT OF CHRIST

## Trumpet

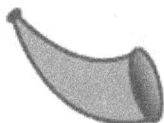

The trumpet is a symbol of the Last Judgment, the resurrection, and the call to worship. Trumpets call to mind the story of Joshua and the battle of Jericho (Joshua 6) and of Gideon against the Midianites (Judges 7). Trumpets are associated in the Old Testament with solemn pronouncements of God or in God's presence, of celebration and praise, and of God's people going into battle.

## Phoenix

An ancient myth held that the beautiful phoenix, which lived in the Arabian desert, lived to be five hundred years old and then set its nest on fire and was consumed in the flames. After three days, the phoenix rose again from the ashes, restored to youth, to live another five hundred years. Early Christians saw in this tale a symbol of the Resurrection. St. Clement related the story during the first century in his first letter to the Corinthians. It was used to symbolize resurrection generally at first, and gradually came to signify the Resurrection of Christ. It may signify the fact that those who fall asleep in Christ shall rise again to newness of life.

# LESSON THIRTEEN

## READING ABOUT ADVENT OF CHRIST

**John 17:6** Ἐφανέρωσά σου τὸ ὄνομα τοῖς ἀνθρώποις οὓς ἔδωκάς μοι ἐκ τοῦ κόσμου.

σοὶ ἦσαν κἀμοὶ αὐτοὺς ἔδωκας καὶ τὸν λόγον σου τετήρηκαν. **7** νῦν ἔγνωκαν ὅτι πάντα

ὅσα δέδωκάς μοι παρὰ σοῦ εἰσιν· **8** ὅτι τὰ ῥήματα ἃ ἔδωκάς μοι δέδωκα αὐτοῖς, καὶ

αὐτοὶ ἔλαβον καὶ ἔγνωσαν ἀληθῶς ὅτι παρὰ σοῦ ἐξῆλθον, καὶ ἐπίστευσαν ὅτι σύ με

ἀπέστειλας. **9** Ἐγὼ περὶ αὐτῶν ἐρωτῶ, οὐ περὶ τοῦ κόσμου ἐρωτῶ ἀλλὰ περὶ ὧν

δέδωκάς μοι, ὅτι σοί εἰσιν, **10** καὶ τὰ ἐμὰ πάντα σά ἐστιν καὶ τὰ σὰ ἐμά, καὶ

δεδόξασμαι ἐν αὐτοῖς. **11** καὶ οὐκέτι εἰμὶ ἐν τῷ κόσμῳ, καὶ αὐτοὶ ἐν τῷ κόσμῳ εἰσίν,

κἀγὼ πρὸς σὲ ἔρχομαι. πάτερ ἅγιε, τήρησον αὐτοὺς ἐν τῷ ὀνόματί σου ᾧ δέδωκάς μοι,

ἵνα ὦσιν ἓν καθὼς ἡμεῖς. **12** ὅτε ἤμην μετ᾽ αὐτῶν ἐγὼ ἐτήρουν αὐτοὺς ἐν τῷ ὀνόματί

σου ᾧ δέδωκάς μοι, καὶ ἐφύλαξα, καὶ οὐδεὶς ἐξ αὐτῶν ἀπώλετο εἰ μὴ ὁ υἱὸς τῆς

ἀπωλείας, ἵνα ἡ γραφὴ πληρωθῇ.

**Matthew 24:15** Ὅταν οὖν ἴδητε τὸ βδέλυγμα τῆς ἐρημώσεως τὸ ῥηθὲν διὰ Δανιὴλ τοῦ

προφήτου ἑστὸς ἐν τόπῳ ἁγίῳ, ὁ ἀναγινώσκων νοείτω, **16** τότε οἱ ἐν τῇ Ἰουδαίᾳ

φευγέτωσαν εἰς τὰ ὄρη, **17** ὁ ἐπὶ τοῦ δώματος μὴ καταβάτω ἆραι τὰ ἐκ τῆς οἰκίας

αὐτοῦ, **18** καὶ ὁ ἐν τῷ ἀγρῷ μὴ ἐπιστρεψάτω ὀπίσω ἆραι τὸ ἱμάτιον αὐτοῦ. **19** οὐαὶ

δὲ ταῖς ἐν γαστρὶ ἐχούσαις καὶ ταῖς θηλαζούσαις ἐν ἐκείναις ταῖς ἡμέραις. **20**

προσεύχεσθε δὲ ἵνα μὴ γένηται ἡ φυγὴ ὑμῶν χειμῶνος μηδὲ σαββάτῳ. **21** ἔσται γὰρ

τότε θλῖψις μεγάλη οἵα οὐ γέγονεν ἀπ᾽ ἀρχῆς κόσμου ἕως τοῦ νῦν οὐδ᾽ οὐ μὴ γένηται.

**22** καὶ εἰ μὴ ἐκολοβώθησαν αἱ ἡμέραι ἐκεῖναι, οὐκ ἂν ἐσώθη πᾶσα σάρξ· διὰ δὲ τοὺς

ἐκλεκτοὺς κολοβωθήσονται αἱ ἡμέραι ἐκεῖναι. **23** Τότε ἐάν τις ὑμῖν εἴπῃ· ἰδοὺ ὧδε ὁ

χριστός, ἤ· ὧδε, μὴ πιστεύσητε· **24** ἐγερθήσονται γὰρ ψευδόχριστοι καὶ ψευδοπροφῆται

καὶ δώσουσιν σημεῖα μεγάλα καὶ τέρατα ὥστε πλανῆσαι, εἰ δυνατόν, καὶ τοὺς

ἐκλεκτούς. **25** ἰδοὺ προείρηκα ὑμῖν. **26** ἐὰν οὖν εἴπωσιν ὑμῖν· ἰδοὺ ἐν τῇ ἐρήμῳ

ἐστίν, μὴ ἐξέλθητε· ἰδοὺ ἐν τοῖς ταμείοις, μὴ πιστεύσητε· **27** ὥσπερ γὰρ ἡ ἀστραπὴ ἐξέρχεται ἀπὸ ἀνατολῶν καὶ φαίνεται ἕως δυσμῶν, οὕτως ἔσται ἡ παρουσία τοῦ υἱοῦ

τοῦ ἀνθρώπου· 28 ὅπου ἐὰν ᾖ τὸ πτῶμα, ἐκεῖ συναχθήσονται οἱ ἀετοί.

**1 Thessalonians 4:13** Οὐ θέλομεν δὲ ὑμᾶς ἀγνοεῖν, ἀδελφοί, περὶ τῶν κοιμωμένων,

ἵνα μὴ λυπῆσθε καθὼς καὶ οἱ λοιποὶ οἱ μὴ ἔχοντες ἐλπίδα. **14** εἰ γὰρ πιστεύομεν ὅτι

Ἰησοῦς ἀπέθανεν καὶ ἀνέστη, οὕτως καὶ ὁ θεὸς τοὺς κοιμηθέντας διὰ τοῦ Ἰησοῦ ἄξει

σὺν αὐτῷ. **15** Τοῦτο γὰρ ὑμῖν λέγομεν ἐν λόγῳ κυρίου, ὅτι ἡμεῖς οἱ ζῶντες οἱ

περιλειπόμενοι εἰς τὴν παρουσίαν τοῦ κυρίου οὐ μὴ φθάσωμεν τοὺς κοιμηθέντας· **16**

ὅτι αὐτὸς ὁ κύριος ἐν κελεύσματι, ἐν φωνῇ ἀρχαγγέλου καὶ ἐν σάλπιγγι θεοῦ,

καταβήσεται ἀπ' οὐρανοῦ καὶ οἱ νεκροὶ ἐν Χριστῷ ἀναστήσονται πρῶτον, **17** ἔπειτα

ἡμεῖς οἱ ζῶντες οἱ περιλειπόμενοι ἅμα σὺν αὐτοῖς ἁρπαγησόμεθα ἐν νεφέλαις εἰς

ἀπάντησιν τοῦ κυρίου εἰς ἀέρα· καὶ οὕτως πάντοτε σὺν κυρίῳ ἐσόμεθα. **18** Ὥστε

παρακαλεῖτε ἀλλήλους ἐν τοῖς λόγοις τούτοις.

......

**1 Thessalonians 5:1** Περὶ δὲ τῶν χρόνων καὶ τῶν καιρῶν, ἀδελφοί, οὐ χρείαν ἔχετε

ὑμῖν γράφεσθαι, **2** αὐτοὶ γὰρ ἀκριβῶς οἴδατε ὅτι ἡμέρα κυρίου ὡς κλέπτης ἐν νυκτὶ

οὕτως ἔρχεται. **3** ὅταν λέγωσιν· εἰρήνη καὶ ἀσφάλεια, τότε αἰφνίδιος αὐτοῖς ἐφίσταται

ὄλεθρος ὥσπερ ἡ ὠδὶν τῇ ἐν γαστρὶ ἐχούσῃ, καὶ οὐ μὴ ἐκφύγωσιν. **4** ὑμεῖς δέ,

ἀδελφοί, οὐκ ἐστὲ ἐν σκότει, ἵνα ἡ ἡμέρα ὑμᾶς ὡς κλέπτης καταλάβῃ· **5** πάντες γὰρ

ὑμεῖς υἱοὶ φωτός ἐστε καὶ υἱοὶ ἡμέρας. Οὐκ ἐσμὲν νυκτὸς οὐδὲ σκότους· **6** ἄρα οὖν μὴ

καθεύδωμεν ὡς οἱ λοιποί ἀλλὰ γρηγορῶμεν καὶ νήφωμεν.

# QUESTIONS FOR HEART AND MIND

## ADVENT OF CHRIST

### MATTHEW 24:15-28

1. Identify six events or characteristics of the end times.

2. Cite two ways to distinguish false christs from Christ.

3. How does verse 15 reflect Jesus' hermeneutic?

    Is he a model for us?  Why or why not?

# QUESTIONS FOR HEART AND MIND

## ADVENT OF CHRIST

### 1 THESSALONIANS 4:13-5:6

1.  List four events marking the return of Christ.

2.  Distinguish the subjects addressed in 4:13-18 and 5:1-6.

3.  What difference does the placing of διὰ τοῦ Ἰησου make in verse 14?

# CLASS DISCUSSION QUESTIONS

## INFINITIVES

## ADVENT OF CHRIST

## MATTHEW 24:15-28

1.  What is the tense and function of the infinitive ἆραι (vv. 17-18)?


    Why would Jesus use this tense and not some other?


2.  What is the tense of the infinitive πλανῆσαι and what are the possible options for the function of it (v. 24)?


    What factors in the context support the observation that the function is that of purpose rather than result?


3.  What is significant about the use of the perfect γέγονεν (v. 21)?


4.  What function is common to the verb forms in verses 27-28?


    How does this relate to the function of the verb form (ἔσται) used to express the coming of the Son of man (v. 27)?


    How do these factors assist in interpreting the meaning of the coming of Christ?

## CLASS DISCUSSION QUESTIONS

## INFINITIVES

### ADVENT OF CHRIST

### 1 THESSALONIANS 4:13-5:6

1. What is the tense and function of the infinitive ἀγνοεῖν (v. 13)?

   What does the tense of the main verb and of the infinitive contribute to the interpretation of the passage?

2. What is the tense and the function of the infinitive γράφεσθαι (5:1)?

   What does the tense of the main verb and of the infinitive contribute to the interpretation of the passage?

3. Compare the infinitives in the constructions of 5:1 with 4:9. What are the differences and what is the possible significance for interpretation?

4. Note the construction of εἰς ἀπάντησιν (v. 17). How might this have been expressed by an infinitive (what tense and function would have been involved)?

   What does this suggest about the function of εἰς ἀπάντησιν here?

5. With what does the prepositional phase διὰ τοῦ Ἰησοῦ go (i.e., What are the options) (v. 14)?

   What are the implications for interpretation?

# INFINITIVES (Verbal Nouns)

| Function | Key Concepts | N.T. Example | B&W | Wall |
|---|---|---|---|---|
| **A. VERBAL (Adverbial)** | | | | |
| 1. Purpose | Aim, Design | Mt.5:17; Lk.2:22 | 133 | 590 |
| 2. Result | Result of action | Ac.5:3; Rom.7:3 | 135 | 592 |
| 3. Time | Relative to verb | | | |
| a. Antecedent | "Before" (πριν) | Jn.4:49; Mk.14:30 | 136 | 594 |
| b. Contemporaneous | "While" (εν τω) | Lk.1:21; Mt.13:4 | 136 | 595 |
| c. Subsequent | "After" (μετα) | Lk.12:5; Ac.1:3 | 137 | 596 |
| d. Future | "Until" (εως) | Ac.8:40 | 137 | -- |
| 4. Cause | "Because" (δια) | Mt.13:6; Jas.4:2 | 138 | 596 |
| 5. Means (rare) | How? (εν τω) | Ac.3:26; 4:29-30 | -- | 597 |
| 6. Command | Imperatival | Phil.3:16; Rom12:15 | 138 | 608 |
| 7. Absolute | Greetings | Ac.15:23; Jas.1:1 | 139 | 608 |
| **B. SUBSTANTIVAL (Noun, Adjective)** | | | | |
| 1. Subject | Subject of verb | Mt.3:15; Phil.1:21 | 139 | 600 |
| 2. Object | | | | |
| a. Direct | Object of verb | Ac.25:11; 2 Cor.8:11 | 140 | 601 |
| b. Indirect Discourse | Verb of saying, etc. | Mk.12:18; Jn.12:29 | 140 | 603 |
| c. Complementary | Completes verb | Heb.7:25; Lk.21:36 | 140 | 598 |
| 3. Modifier | | | | |
| a. Of Substantives | Adjective or Apposition | Mt.3:14; Jas.1:27 | 141 | 606 |
| b. Of Verbs? | Epexegetical | Rom.1:24; 1:28 | 142 | 607 |

# ASSIGNMENT

## IDENTIFY SYNTACTICAL FORMS/FUNCTIONS

## INFINITIVES

## MATTHEW 24:15-28

A. Identify the infinitive and its function
   1. ἆραι  (v. 17)                    2. πλανῆσαι  (v. 24)

B. Identify the tense and its function
   1. ἴδητε  (v. 15)                   5. δώσουσιν  (v. 24)

   2. ἔσται  (v. 21)                   6. προείρηκα  (v. 25)

   3. γέγονεν                          7. ἐστίν  (v. 26)

   4. ἐσώθη  (v. 22)                   8. ἐξέρχεται  (v. 27)

C. Identify the mood and its function
   1. ἴδητε  (v. 15)                   6. γένηται  (v. 21)

   2. νοείτω                           7. εἴπῃ  (v. 23)

   3. φευγέτωσαν  (v. 16)              8. πιστεύσητε

   4. προσεύχεσθε  (v. 20)             9. εἴπωσιν  (v. 26)

   5. γένηται                          10. ᾖ  (v. 28)

D. Identify the case and its function
   1. ἐρημώσεως  (v. 15)               6. σαββάτῳ

   2. προφήτου                         7. κόσμου  (v. 21)

   3. ἱμάτιον  (v. 18)                 8. χριστός  (v. 23)

   4. ἐχούσαις  (v. 19                 9. υἱοῦ  (v. 27)

   5. χειμῶνος  (v. 20)               10. ἀνθρώπου

# ASSIGNMENT

# IDENTIFY SYNTACTICAL FORMS/FUNCTIONS

## INFINITIVES

### 1 THESSALONIANS 4:13-5:6

A.  Identify the infinitive and its function
    1.  ἀγνοεῖν (v. 13)             2.  γράφεσθαι (5:1)

B.  Identify the case and its function

| | |
|---|---|
| 1.  ὑμᾶς (v. 13) | 11. κυρίου (v. 17) |
| 2.  ἀδελφοί | 12. λόγοις (v. 18) |
| 3.  ἐλπίδα | 13. ὑμῖν (5:1) |
| 4.  Ἰησοῦς (v. 14) | 14. κυρίου (v. 2) |
| 5.  Ἰησοῦ | 15. κλέπτης |
| 6.  αὐτῷ | 16. Εἰρήνη (v. 3) |
| 7.  Τοῦτο (v. 15) | 17. ὠδὶν |
| 8.  κυρίου (1st) | 18. υἱοὶ (v. 5) |
| 9.  κυρίου (2nd) | 19. φωτός |
| 10. θεοῦ (v. 16) | 20. νυκτὸς |

C.  Identify the tense and its function

| | |
|---|---|
| 1.  λυπῆσθε (v. 13) | 10. οἴδατε (v. 2) |
| 2.  πιστεύομεν (v. 14) | 11. ἔρχεται |
| 3.  ἀπέθανεν | 12. λέγωσιν (v. 3) |
| 4.  ἄξει | 13. ἐφίσταται |
| 5.  φθάσωμεν (v. 15) | 14. ἐκφύγωσιν |
| 6.  καταβήσεται (v. 16) | 15. ἐστὲ (v. 4) |
| 7.  ἁρπαγησόμεθα (v. 17) | 16. ἐστὲ (v. 5) |
| 8.  παρακαλεῖτε (v. 18) | 17. καθεύδωμεν (v. 6) |
| 9.  ἔχετε (5:1) | 18. γρηγορῶμεν |

# LESSON FOURTEEN:
# SYMBOLISM ABOUT CHRIST/NAME

## Chi Rho

The Chi Rho is one of the most ancient "sacred monograms" of Christ. They were developed by early Christians as a secret sign of their faith. This monogram is composed of the first two Greek letters of the word "Christ" (XPICTOC). The Chi Rho has many variations.

This Chi Rho appears with the Alpha and Omega, the first and last letters of the Greek alphabet.

Rev. 22:13 I am the Alpha and the Omega, the First and the Last, the Beginning and the End. *(NIV)*

This style incorporates an anchor cross. The anchor represents the hope that we have in Christ.

Hebr. 6:17 Because God wanted to make the unchanging nature of his purpose very clear to the heirs of what was promised, he confirmed it with an oath. 18 God did this so that, by two unchangeable things in which it is impossible for God to lie, we who have fled to take hold of the hope offered to us may be greatly encouraged. 19 We have this hope as an anchor for the soul, firm and secure. It enters the inner sanctuary behind the curtain, 20 where Jesus, who went before us, has entered on our behalf. He has become a high priest forever, in the order of Melchizedek. *(NIV)*

This unusual style makes a "P" of one of the arms of the "X," rather than vice versa. The short wavy bar is the symbol for an abbreviation.

# LESSON FOURTEEN
## READING ABOUT CHRIST/NAME

**John 17:13** νῦν δὲ πρὸς σὲ ἔρχομαι καὶ ταῦτα λαλῶ ἐν τῷ κόσμῳ ἵνα ἔχωσιν τὴν χαρὰν τὴν ἐμὴν πεπληρωμένην ἐν ἑαυτοῖς. **14** ἐγὼ δέδωκα αὐτοῖς τὸν λόγον σου καὶ ὁ κόσμος ἐμίσησεν αὐτούς, ὅτι οὐκ εἰσὶν ἐκ τοῦ κόσμου καθὼς ἐγὼ οὐκ εἰμὶ ἐκ τοῦ κόσμου. **15** οὐκ ἐρωτῶ ἵνα ἄρῃς αὐτοὺς ἐκ τοῦ κόσμου, ἀλλ' ἵνα τηρήσῃς αὐτοὺς ἐκ τοῦ πονηροῦ. **16** ἐκ τοῦ κόσμου οὐκ εἰσὶν καθὼς ἐγὼ οὐκ εἰμὶ ἐκ τοῦ κόσμου. **17** ἁγίασον αὐτοὺς ἐν τῇ ἀληθείᾳ· ὁ λόγος ὁ σὸς ἀλήθειά ἐστιν. **18** καθὼς ἐμὲ ἀπέστειλας εἰς τὸν κόσμον, κἀγὼ ἀπέστειλα αὐτοὺς εἰς τὸν κόσμον· **19** καὶ ὑπὲρ αὐτῶν ἐγὼ ἁγιάζω ἐμαυτόν, ἵνα ὦσιν καὶ αὐτοὶ ἡγιασμένοι ἐν ἀληθείᾳ.

**Philippians 2:1** Εἴ τις οὖν παράκλησις ἐν Χριστῷ, εἴ τι παραμύθιον ἀγάπης, εἴ τις κοινωνία πνεύματος, εἴ τις σπλάγχνα καὶ οἰκτιρμοί, **2** πληρώσατέ μου τὴν χαρὰν ἵνα τὸ αὐτὸ φρονῆτε, τὴν αὐτὴν ἀγάπην ἔχοντες, σύμψυχοι, τὸ ἓν φρονοῦντες, **3** μηδὲν κατ' ἐριθείαν μηδὲ κατὰ κενοδοξίαν ἀλλὰ τῇ ταπεινοφροσύνῃ ἀλλήλους ἡγούμενοι ὑπερέχοντας ἑαυτῶν, **4** μὴ τὰ ἑαυτῶν ἕκαστος σκοποῦντες ἀλλὰ [καὶ] τὰ ἑτέρων

ἕκαστοι. **5** Τοῦτο φρονεῖτε ἐν ὑμῖν ὃ καὶ ἐν Χριστῷ Ἰησοῦ, **6** ὃς ἐν μορφῇ θεοῦ

ὑπάρχων οὐχ ἁρπαγμὸν ἡγήσατο τὸ εἶναι ἴσα θεῷ, **7** ἀλλὰ ἑαυτὸν ἐκένωσεν μορφὴν

δούλου λαβών, ἐν ὁμοιώματι ἀνθρώπων γενόμενος· καὶ σχήματι εὑρεθεὶς ὡς ἄνθρωπος

**8** ἐταπείνωσεν ἑαυτὸν γενόμενος ὑπήκοος μέχρι θανάτου, θανάτου δὲ σταυροῦ. **9** διὸ

καὶ ὁ θεὸς αὐτὸν ὑπερύψωσεν καὶ ἐχαρίσατο αὐτῷ τὸ ὄνομα τὸ ὑπὲρ πᾶν ὄνομα, **10**

ἵνα ἐν τῷ ὀνόματι Ἰησοῦ πᾶν γόνυ κάμψῃ ἐπουρανίων καὶ ἐπιγείων καὶ καταχθονίων

**11** καὶ πᾶσα γλῶσσα ἐξομολογήσηται ὅτι κύριος Ἰησοῦς Χριστὸς εἰς δόξαν θεοῦ

πατρός.

**Revelation 19:11** Καὶ εἶδον τὸν οὐρανὸν ἠνεῳγμένον, καὶ ἰδοὺ ἵππος λευκός καὶ ὁ

καθήμενος ἐπ᾽ αὐτὸν [καλούμενος] πιστὸς καὶ ἀληθινός, καὶ ἐν δικαιοσύνῃ κρίνει καὶ

πολεμεῖ. **12** οἱ δὲ ὀφθαλμοὶ αὐτοῦ [ὡς] φλὸξ πυρός, καὶ ἐπὶ τὴν κεφαλὴν αὐτοῦ

διαδήματα πολλά, ἔχων ὄνομα γεγραμμένον ὃ οὐδεὶς οἶδεν εἰ μὴ αὐτός, **13** καὶ

περιβεβλημένος ἱμάτιον βεβαμμένον αἵματι, καὶ κέκληται τὸ ὄνομα αὐτοῦ ὁ λόγος τοῦ

θεοῦ. **14** Καὶ τὰ στρατεύματα [τὰ] ἐν τῷ οὐρανῷ ἠκολούθει αὐτῷ ἐφ᾽ ἵπποις λευκοῖς, ἐνδεδυμένοι βύσσινον λευκὸν καθαρόν. **15** καὶ ἐκ τοῦ στόματος αὐτοῦ ἐκπορεύεται

ῥομφαία ὀξεῖα, ἵνα ἐν αὐτῇ πατάξῃ τὰ ἔθνη, καὶ αὐτὸς ποιμανεῖ αὐτοὺς ἐν ῥάβδῳ

σιδηρᾷ, καὶ αὐτὸς πατεῖ τὴν ληνὸν τοῦ οἴνου τοῦ θυμοῦ τῆς ὀργῆς τοῦ θεοῦ τοῦ

παντοκράτορος, **16** καὶ ἔχει ἐπὶ τὸ ἱμάτιον καὶ ἐπὶ τὸν μηρὸν αὐτοῦ ὄνομα

γεγραμμένον· Βασιλεὺς βασιλέων καὶ κύριος κυρίων. **17** Καὶ εἶδον ἕνα ἄγγελον

ἑστῶτα ἐν τῷ ἡλίῳ καὶ ἔκραξεν [ἐν] φωνῇ μεγάλῃ λέγων πᾶσιν τοῖς ὀρνέοις τοῖς

πετομένοις ἐν μεσουρανήματι· Δεῦτε συνάχθητε εἰς τὸ δεῖπνον τὸ μέγα τοῦ θεοῦ **18**

ἵνα φάγητε σάρκας βασιλέων καὶ σάρκας χιλιάρχων καὶ σάρκας ἰσχυρῶν καὶ σάρκας

ἵππων καὶ τῶν καθημένων ἐπ᾽ αὐτῶν καὶ σάρκας πάντων ἐλευθέρων τε καὶ δούλων καὶ

μικρῶν καὶ μεγάλων. **19** Καὶ εἶδον τὸ θηρίον καὶ τοὺς βασιλεῖς τῆς γῆς καὶ τὰ

στρατεύματα αὐτῶν συνηγμένα ποιῆσαι τὸν πόλεμον μετὰ τοῦ καθημένου ἐπὶ τοῦ ἵππου

καὶ μετὰ τοῦ στρατεύματος αὐτοῦ. **20** καὶ ἐπιάσθη τὸ θηρίον καὶ μετ᾽ αὐτοῦ ὁ

ψευδοπροφήτης ὁ ποιήσας τὰ σημεῖα ἐνώπιον αὐτοῦ, ἐν οἷς ἐπλάνησεν τοὺς λαβόντας τὸ

χάραγμα τοῦ θηρίου καὶ τοὺς προσκυνοῦντας τῇ εἰκόνι αὐτοῦ· ζῶντες ἐβλήθησαν οἱ δύο

εἰς τὴν λίμνην τοῦ πυρὸς τῆς καιομένης ἐν θείῳ.

# QUESTIONS FOR HEART AND MIND

## CHRIST/NAME

## PHILIPPIANS 2:1-11

1.  In what ways did Christ humble himself?

2.  Why does Paul pen these words about the humiliation of Christ?

3.  Of what did Christ "empty" himself (v. 7)?

4.  What is the name "above every name"?

## QUESTIONS FOR HEART AND MIND

### CHRIST/NAME

### REVELATION 19:11-19

1. By what three general ways is the rider on the white horse identified as Christ?

2. List five events which accompany the return of Christ.

3. Cite three examples of lack of agreement (concord) in grammar.

# CLASS DISCUSSION QUESTIONS

## PARTICIPLES

## CHRIST/NAME

## PHILIPPIANS 2:1-11

1. What verbal connection exists between Philippians 2:6 and 1 Thessalonians 4:17?

2. What is the use of the infinitive εἶναι (v. 6)?

    How do the words ἴσα θεῷ function? What cases are they in?

    How does the clause τὸ εἶναι ἴσα θεῷ function? In what case is the infinitive?

    What is the case and function of ἁρπαγμὸν?

    What is the function of the participle ὑπάρχων?

    How does the meaning of the syntax of this verse help to explain the meaning of ἐκένωσεν (v. 7)?

3. How have the participles of verses 7-8 contributed to the confusion over where to begin verse 8?

    What is the function of the participles of verses 7-8?

    How important to the interpretation of this passage are the participles?

4. What is the verbal connection between this passage and Revelation 19:11-20?

# CLASS DISCUSSION QUESTIONS

## PARTICIPLES

## CHRIST/NAME

## REVELATION 19:11-19

1. How does the grammar/syntax of this apocalypse genre differ from the genre of epistle and narrative (gospel)?

2. Cite some examples of solecisms or ungrammatical forms (vv. 11-16). In each case identify what makes them ungrammatical?

3. Identify the function of the five nouns in the genitive form at the end of verse 15.

4. What is the import of the fivefold repetition of σάρκας (v. 18)?

# PARTICIPLES  (Verbal Adjectives)

| Function | Key Concepts | N.T. Example | B&W | Wall |
|---|---|---|---|---|
| **A. ADJECTIVAL  (As Adjective or Noun)** | | | | |
| 1. Attributive | Modifies noun | Phil.4:7; Ac.10:1 | 143 | 617 |
| 2. Substantival | As a noun | Mt.10:37; Phil.3:17 | 144 | 619 |
| 3. Predicative | Linking verb | | | |
|   a. Predicate Adj. | Additional assertion | Gal.1:22; Rev.1:18 | 144 | 618 |
|   b. Periphrastic | Completes verb | Lk.11:14; 20:6 | 144 | 647 |
| **B. ADVERBIAL  (As Adverb)** | | | | |
| 1. Temporal | Relative time ("when") | Rom.4:10; 2 Cor.2:13 | 146 | 623 |
| 2. Telic | Purpose ("in order to") | Ac.3:26; 8:27 | 147 | 635 |
| 3. Causal | Reason ("because, since") | 1 Tim.4:8; Lk.23:20 | 147 | 631 |
| 4. Conditional | ("If") | Heb.2:3; Gal.6:9 | 148 | 632 |
| 5. Concessive | ("Although") | Heb.5:12; Phil.2:6 | 148 | 634 |
| 6. Instrumental, Means | Means ("by") | Mt.6:27; Lk.15:13 | 149 | 628 |
| 7. Modal, Manner | Manner ("by") | Mt.19:22; Lk.1:64 | 150 | 627 |
| 8. Complementary | Completes verb | Mt.11:1; 6:16 | 150 | 646 |
|   (Supplement.) | Indirect discourse | 3 Jn.4; 1 Jn.4:2 | 150 | 645 |
| 9. Circumstantial, | Incidental ("and"+verb) | Lk.4:15; Mk.1:7 | 151 | 640 |
|     Absolute | Noun & ptc. in gen case | Mt.9:18; Rom.7:3 | 151 | 655 |
| 10. Imperatival | Command | Rom.12:9; 1 Pet.3:1 | 152 | 650 |

# ASSIGNMENT

## IDENTIFY SYNTACTICAL FORMS/FUNCTIONS

### PARTICIPLES

### PHILIPPIANS 2:1-11

A.  Identify the verbal form (infinitive or participle) and its function
1. ἔχοντες (v. 2)                    7. εἶναι

2. φρονοῦντες                        8. λαβών (v. 7)

3. ἡγούμενοι (v. 3)                  9. γενόμενος

4. ὑπερέχοντας                       10. εὑρεθεὶς

5. σκοποῦντες (v. 4)                 11. γενόμενος (v. 8)

6. ὑπάρχων (v. 6)

B.  Identify the case and its function
1. παραμύθιον (v. 1)          15. ἴσα
2. ἀγάπης                     16. θεῷ
3. πνεύματος                  17. δούλου (v. 7)
4. αὐτὸ (v. 2)                18. ὁμοιώματι
5. σύμψυχοι                   19. ἀνθρώπων
6. μηδὲν (v. 3)               20. σχήματι
7. ταπεινοφροσύνῃ             21. ἄνθρωπος
8. ἀλλήλους                   22. ὑπήκοος (v. 8)
9. ὑπερέχοντας                23. θανάτου (2nd)
10. ἑαυτῶν                    24. σταυροῦ
11. ἑαυτῶν (v. 4)             25. αὐτῷ (v. 9)
12. θεοῦ (v. 6)               26. Ἰησοῦ (v. 10)
13. ἁρπαγμὸν                  27. κύριος (v. 11)
14. τὸ εἶναι                  28. Ἰησοῦς

C.  Identify the use of the article
1. τὸ (v. 2)                  3. τὸ (v. 6)
2. τῇ (v. 3)                  4. τὸ (2nd; v. 9)

# ASSIGNMENT

## IDENTIFY SYNTACTICAL FORMS/FUNCTIONS

## PARTICIPLES

## REVELATION 19:11-19

A.  Identify the verbal form (infinitive or participle) and its function

| | |
|---|---|
| 1.  ἠνεῳγμένον (v. 11) | 8.  πετομένοις |
| 2.  καθήμενος | 9.  καθημένων  (v. 18) |
| 3.  ἔχων  (v. 12) | 10.  συνηγμένα  (v. 19) |
| 4.  γεγραμμένον | 11.  ποιῆσαι |
| 5.  περιβεβλημένος  (v. 13) | 12.  ποιήσας  (v. 20) |
| 6.  ἐνδεδυμένοι  (v. 14) | 13.  λαβόντας  (v. 20) |
| 7.  ἑστῶτα  (v. 17) | 14.  ζῶντες |

B.  Identify the case and its function

| | |
|---|---|
| 1.  ἵππος (v. 11) | 13.  ῥάβδῳ |
| 2.  πιστὸς | 14.  οἴνου |
| 3.  ὀφθαλμοὶ  (v. 12) | 15.  Θυμοῦ |
| 4.  πυρός | 16.  ὀργῆς |
| 5.  διαδήματα | 17.  θεοῦ |
| 6.  ὄνομα | 18.  Βασιλεὺς  (v. 16) |
| 7.  αἵματι  (v. 13) | 19.  βασιλέων |
| 8.  λόγος | 20.  φωνῇ  (v. 17) |
| 9.  θεοῦ | 21.  ὀρνέοις |
| 10.  αὐτῷ  (v. 14) | 22.  βασιλέων  (v. 18) |
| 11.  βύσσινον | 23.  πόλεμον  (v. 19) |
| 12.  στόματος  (v. 15) | 24.  θηρίου  (v. 20) |

C.  Identify the tense and its function

| | |
|---|---|
| 1.  κρίνει  (v. 11) | 5.  ποιμανεῖ |
| 2.  κέκληται  (v. 13) | 6.  ἔκραξεν  (v. 17) |
| 3.  ἠκολούθει  (v. 14) | 7.  ἐπιάσθη  (v. 20) |
| 4.  ἐκπορεύεται  (v. 15) | 8.  ἐπλάνησεν |

# LESSON FIFTEEN:
# SYMBOLISM ABOUT UNION WITH CHRIST/HOLINESS

Fish with the Anchor

The fish was frequently found with an anchor, another 1st century Christian symbol. The symbol would then mean that Jesus, being God's Son and the person's Savior, is the unmoving anchor of the person's life. No matter what happens in life the person is secure in                                                                                               Christ.

# LESSON FIFTEEN

## READING ABOUT UNION WITH CHRIST/HOLINESS

**John 17:20** Οὐ περὶ τούτων δὲ ἐρωτῶ μόνον, ἀλλὰ καὶ περὶ τῶν πιστευόντων διὰ τοῦ

λόγου αὐτῶν εἰς ἐμέ, **21** ἵνα πάντες ἓν ὦσιν, καθὼς σύ, πάτερ, ἐν ἐμοὶ κἀγὼ ἐν σοί,

ἵνα καὶ αὐτοὶ ἐν ἡμῖν ὦσιν, ἵνα ὁ κόσμος πιστεύῃ ὅτι σύ με ἀπέστειλας. **22** κἀγὼ τὴν

δόξαν ἣν δέδωκάς μοι δέδωκα αὐτοῖς, ἵνα ὦσιν ἓν καθὼς ἡμεῖς ἕν· **23** ἐγὼ ἐν αὐτοῖς

καὶ σὺ ἐν ἐμοί, ἵνα ὦσιν τετελειωμένοι εἰς ἕν, ἵνα γινώσκῃ ὁ κόσμος ὅτι σύ με

ἀπέστειλας καὶ ἠγάπησας αὐτοὺς καθὼς ἐμὲ ἠγάπησας. **24** Πάτερ, ὃ δέδωκάς μοι, θέλω

ἵνα ὅπου εἰμὶ ἐγὼ κἀκεῖνοι ὦσιν μετ᾽ ἐμοῦ, ἵνα θεωρῶσιν τὴν δόξαν τὴν ἐμήν, ἣν

δέδωκάς μοι ὅτι ἠγάπησάς με πρὸ καταβολῆς κόσμου. **25** πάτερ δίκαιε, καὶ ὁ κόσμος σε

οὐκ ἔγνω, ἐγὼ δέ σε ἔγνων, καὶ οὗτοι ἔγνωσαν ὅτι σύ με ἀπέστειλας· **26** καὶ

ἐγνώρισα αὐτοῖς τὸ ὄνομά σου καὶ γνωρίσω, ἵνα ἡ ἀγάπη ἣν ἠγάπησάς με ἐν αὐτοῖς ᾖ

κἀγὼ ἐν αὐτοῖς.

**Romans 6:1** Τί οὖν ἐροῦμεν; ἐπιμένωμεν τῇ ἁμαρτίᾳ, ἵνα ἡ χάρις πλεονάσῃ; **2** μὴ

γένοιτο. οἵτινες ἀπεθάνομεν τῇ ἁμαρτίᾳ, πῶς ἔτι ζήσομεν ἐν αὐτῇ; **3** ἢ ἀγνοεῖτε ὅτι, ὅσοι ἐβαπτίσθημεν εἰς Χριστὸν Ἰησοῦν, εἰς τὸν θάνατον αὐτοῦ ἐβαπτίσθημεν; **4**

συνετάφημεν οὖν αὐτῷ διὰ τοῦ βαπτίσματος εἰς τὸν θάνατον, ἵνα ὥσπερ ἠγέρθη

Χριστὸς ἐκ νεκρῶν διὰ τῆς δόξης τοῦ πατρός, οὕτως καὶ ἡμεῖς ἐν καινότητι ζωῆς

περιπατήσωμεν. **5** εἰ γὰρ σύμφυτοι γεγόναμεν τῷ ὁμοιώματι τοῦ θανάτου αὐτοῦ, ἀλλὰ

καὶ τῆς ἀναστάσεως ἐσόμεθα· **6** τοῦτο γινώσκοντες ὅτι ὁ παλαιὸς ἡμῶν ἄνθρωπος

συνεσταυρώθη, ἵνα καταργηθῇ τὸ σῶμα τῆς ἁμαρτίας, τοῦ μηκέτι δουλεύειν ἡμᾶς τῇ

ἁμαρτίᾳ· **7** ὁ γὰρ ἀποθανὼν δεδικαίωται ἀπὸ τῆς ἁμαρτίας. **8** εἰ δὲ ἀπεθάνομεν σὺν

Χριστῷ, πιστεύομεν ὅτι καὶ συζήσομεν αὐτῷ, **9** εἰδότες ὅτι Χριστὸς ἐγερθεὶς ἐκ

νεκρῶν οὐκέτι ἀποθνήσκει, θάνατος αὐτοῦ οὐκέτι κυριεύει. **10** ὃ γὰρ ἀπέθανεν, τῇ

ἁμαρτίᾳ ἀπέθανεν ἐφάπαξ· ὃ δὲ ζῇ, ζῇ τῷ θεῷ. **11** οὕτως καὶ ὑμεῖς λογίζεσθε ἑαυτοὺς

[εἶναι] νεκροὺς μὲν τῇ ἁμαρτίᾳ ζῶντας δὲ τῷ θεῷ ἐν Χριστῷ Ἰησοῦ.


**1 Thessalonians 4:1** Λοιπὸν οὖν, ἀδελφοί, ἐρωτῶμεν ὑμᾶς καὶ παρακαλοῦμεν ἐν

κυρίῳ Ἰησοῦ, ἵνα καθὼς παρελάβετε παρ' ἡμῶν τὸ πῶς δεῖ ὑμᾶς περιπατεῖν καὶ

ἀρέσκειν θεῷ, καθὼς καὶ περιπατεῖτε, ἵνα περισσεύητε μᾶλλον. **2** οἴδατε γὰρ τίνας παραγγελίας ἐδώκαμεν ὑμῖν διὰ τοῦ κυρίου Ἰησοῦ. **3** Τοῦτο γάρ ἐστιν θέλημα τοῦ

θεοῦ, ὁ ἁγιασμὸς ὑμῶν, ἀπέχεσθαι ὑμᾶς ἀπὸ τῆς πορνείας, **4** εἰδέναι ἕκαστον ὑμῶν τὸ

ἑαυτοῦ σκεῦος κτᾶσθαι ἐν ἁγιασμῷ καὶ τιμῇ, **5** μὴ ἐν πάθει ἐπιθυμίας καθάπερ καὶ τὰ

ἔθνη τὰ μὴ εἰδότα τὸν θεόν, **6** τὸ μὴ ὑπερβαίνειν καὶ πλεονεκτεῖν ἐν τῷ πράγματι τὸν

ἀδελφὸν αὐτοῦ, διότι ἔκδικος κύριος περὶ πάντων τούτων, καθὼς καὶ προείπαμεν ὑμῖν

καὶ διεμαρτυράμεθα. **7** οὐ γὰρ ἐκάλεσεν ἡμᾶς ὁ θεὸς ἐπὶ ἀκαθαρσίᾳ ἀλλ' ἐν ἁγιασμῷ. **8**

τοιγαροῦν ὁ ἀθετῶν οὐκ ἄνθρωπον ἀθετεῖ ἀλλὰ τὸν θεὸν τὸν [καὶ] διδόντα τὸ πνεῦμα

αὐτοῦ τὸ ἅγιον εἰς ὑμᾶς. **9** Περὶ δὲ τῆς φιλαδελφίας οὐ χρείαν ἔχετε γράφειν ὑμῖν,

αὐτοὶ γὰρ ὑμεῖς θεοδίδακτοί ἐστε εἰς τὸ ἀγαπᾶν ἀλλήλους, **10** καὶ γὰρ ποιεῖτε αὐτὸ

εἰς πάντας τοὺς ἀδελφοὺς [τοὺς] ἐν ὅλῃ τῇ Μακεδονίᾳ. Παρακαλοῦμεν δὲ ὑμᾶς, ἀδελφοί,

περισσεύειν μᾶλλον **11** καὶ φιλοτιμεῖσθαι ἡσυχάζειν καὶ πράσσειν τὰ ἴδια καὶ

ἐργάζεσθαι ταῖς [ἰδίαις] χερσὶν ὑμῶν, καθὼς ὑμῖν παρηγγείλαμεν, **12** ἵνα περιπατῆτε

εὐσχημόνως πρὸς τοὺς ἔξω καὶ μηδενὸς χρείαν ἔχητε.

# QUESTIONS FOR HEART AND MIND

## UNION WITH CHRIST/HOLINESS

### ROMANS 6:1-11

1. Give three expressions describing the basis of our victory over sin.

2. What is the significance of the present tense of the verb in verse 11?

3. What is the significance of the aorist forms for "die" as used with "sin"?

4. What is the significance of the conditional sentences in verses 5 and 8?

# QUESTIONS FOR HEART AND MIND

## UNION WITH CHRIST/HOLINESS

### 1 THESSALONIANS 4:1-12

1. List three negative traits which define holiness.

2. Give three reasons for pursuing holiness.

3. What evidence is there that holiness is never done in one's lifetime?

# CLASS DISCUSSION QUESTIONS

## INFINITIVES, PARTICIPLES, CONJUNCTIONS

## UNION WITH CHRIST/HOLINESS

## ROMANS 6:1-11

1.   What is the significance (kind and meaning) of the conjunction οὖν (6:1)?

     What is the basis in the preceding context from which the inference is drawn?

     How do the tenses and the use of the ἵνα contribute to the force of
     the inference?

     Find three ways or answers in the context to correct the inference (vv. 1-11).

2.   What kind of conjunction is ἵνα and what is its function (v. 6)?

3.   What category and function is δουλεύειν (v. 6)?

4.   Is the aorist the "once-for-all" tense (cf. v. 10)?  Explain your answer.

5.   Comment on the terms and tenses of verse 11.

# CLASS DISCUSSION QUESTIONS

## CONJUNCTIONS/CLAUSES

## UNION WITH CHRIST/HOLINESS

## 1 THESSALONIANS 4:1-12

1. What is the indicator that this passage is connected to the preceding text, and what is the sense of the connection (v. 1)? That is, what kind of conjunction is present and what idea does it express?

2. How are the two examples of the ἵνα used (v. 1)?

3. There are four different kinds of subordinate clauses. From this passage identify an example of three of them (vv. 1-12). In each case give the use (as a noun, adjective, or adverb) of the subordinate clause cited.

   Which kind of subordinate clause is not used?

4. List all the conjunctions, identify as coordinate or subordinate, and give the function, i.e., the idea expressed, by each (vv. 1-12).

# CONJUNCTIONS AND CLAUSES

## I. DEFINITIONS AND DISTINCTIONS

A.   A conjunction is a word that connects words, phrases, clauses and sentences.

B.   Conjunctions may have several meanings.

C.   Conjunctions are a kind of particle.

D.   Particles include the following kinds:

1.   Intensive (or emphatic):
γε, δη, ει μην, νη, μεν, περ, τοι, και, ουν, ποτε, ναι, που, πως, αμην , αν, μεντοι

2.   Negative:  ου, μη, μη ου, ου μη

3.   Interrogative:  ου, αρα, τις, αρα, γαρ, ουν, τι

4.   Conjunctions:  (see below)

5.   Interjections:  ιδε, δευρο, ιδου, ουα, ουαι, ω, ως, τι

## II. KINDS OF CONJUNCTIONS

A.   **Paratactic (coordinate) Conjunctions:**  connect words, phrases or clauses of equal rank

1.   Copulative (connective):  τε, δε, αλλα, και (as adjunctive, "also"; as ascensive, "even"; as a connective, "and"); ουδε, μηδε, ουτε, μητε

2.   Adversative (contrastive):
δε, αλλα, πλην, μεντοι, ομως, και, μεν, ει μη, καιτοι, ουν, καιτοιγε

3.   Disjunctive:  η, ειτε . . . ειτε, ουτε . . . ουτε

4.   Inferential (illative):  αρα, γαρ, ουν, δη, νυν, τοινυν, ωστε

5.   Causal:  γαρ

      6.   Correlative: μεν . . . δε, και . . . και

      7.   Explanatory: γαρ

      8.   Transitional: δε, ουν

  **B.**  **Hypotactic (subordinate) Conjunctions:** connect clauses which are subordinate to (dependent on) the rest of the sentence.

      1.   Causal: οτι, διο, διοτι, ως, διοπερ, καθως, γαρ, επει, επειδη

      2.   Comparative: ως, καθως, καθοτι, ωσει, ον τροπον, ωσπερ, καθαπερ

      3.   Conditional: ει, εαν, αν, ειπερ, επει? (cf. Chart, Wall, 689).

      4.   Concessive: καιπερ, και ει, ει και, εαν και, καν

      5.   Relative: ος, οστις (and all of the forms of their declensions)

      6.   Result: ωστε, ινα, ως, οτι, οπως?

      7.   Purpose: ινα, οπως, μη after verbs of fearing, ως

      8.   Temporal: οτε, οταν, αχρι, μεχρις, ως, εως, πριν, επει, επειδη

      9.   Local: οπου, ου, οθεν

      10. Declarative: οτι, ινα, ω

**III.**    **FOUR KINDS OF CONSTRUCTIONS OF SUBORDINATE CLAUSES** (see Wallace, 659)

  A. Infinitival:  involve an infinitive

  B. Participial:  involve a participle

  C. Conjunctive:  introduced by a subordinate conjunction

  D. Relative:  introduced by a relative pronoun (ος), a relative adjective (οιος, οσος), or a relative adverb (οπου, οτε)

**IV.   THREE SYNTACTICAL FUNCTIONS (USES) OF SUBORDINATE CLAUSES**
(see Wallace, 660)

A.  Substantival:  subject, predicate nominative, direct object, indirect object, indirect discourse, apposition

B.  Adjectival:  modify a noun, pronoun, or other substantive

C.  Adverbial:  cause, comparison, concession, condition, complement, location, manner, means, purpose, result, time

# ASSIGNMENT

## IDENTIFY SYNTACTICAL FORMS/FUNCTIONS

## CONJUNCTIONS/CLAUSES

### ROMANS 6:1-11

A. Identify the kind of conjunction and its function

1. οὖν  (v. 1)

2. ἵνα

3. ἤ  (v. 3)

4. ὅτι

5. οὖν  (v. 4)

6. ἵνα

7. ὥσπερ

8. οὕτως

9. εἰ  (v. 5)

10. γὰρ

11. ὅτι  (v. 6)

12. ἵνα

13. γὰρ  (v. 7)

14. εἰ  (v. 8)

15. ὅτι

16. ὅτι  (v. 9)

17. γὰρ  (v. 10)

18. δὲ

19. οὕτως  (v. 11)

20. δὲ

B. Identify the verbal form (infinitive or participle) and its function

1. γινώσκοντες  (v. 6)

2. δουλεύειν

3. ἀποθανὼν  (v. 7)

C. Identify the tense and its function

1. ἀπεθάνομεν  (v. 2)

2. ζήσομεν

3. ἠγέρθη  (v. 4)

4. γεγόναμεν  (v. 5)

D. Identify the case and its function

1. αὐτῷ  (v. 4)

2. ζωῆς

3. ὁμοιώματι  (v. 5)

## ASSIGNMENT
### IDENTIFY SYNTACTICAL FORMS/FUNCTIONS

### REVIEW

### I THESSALONIANS 4:1-12

A. Identify the verbal form (infinitive or participle) and its function

1. περιπατεῖν (v. 1)

2. ἀπέχεσθαι (v. 3)

3. εἰδέναι (v. 4)

4. εἰδότα (v. 5)

5. ὑπερβαίνειν (v. 6)

6. ἀθετῶν (v. 8)

7. διδόντα (v. 8)

8. γράφειν (v. 9)

9. ἀγαπᾶν

10. περισσεύειν (v. 10)

11. πράσσειν (v. 11)

B. Identify the case and its function
1. ὑμᾶς (v. 1)

2. Ἰησοῦ

3. ὑμᾶς

4. ὑμῖν (v. 2)

5. θέλημα (v. 3)

6. ἁγιασμὸς

7. ὑμᾶς

8. σκεῦος (v. 4)

9. ἐπιθυμίας (v. 5)

10. ἔθνη

11. ἔκδικος (v. 6)

12. πνεῦμα (v. 8)

13. ὑμῖν (v. 9)

14. θεοδίδακτοί

15. ἀδελφοί (v. 10)

16. χερσὶν (v. 11)

17. ὑμῖν

18. μηδενὸς (v. 12)

C. Identify the tense and its function
1. ἐρωτῶμεν (v. 1)
2. περιπατεῖτε
3. ἐστιν (v. 3)
4. προείπαμεν (v. 6)

5. ἐκάλεσεν (v. 7)
6. ἀθετεῖ (v. 8)
7. ἐστε (v. 9)
8. Παρακαλοῦμεν (v. 10)

# APPENDIX


# *GREEK SYNTAX*


# *QUICK REFERENCE GUIDES*


**Based on Numerous Grammars
(Dana & Mantey, A.T. Robertson, Blass-Debrunner-Funk, Turner, Smyth, etc.)
and Keyed to Brooks & Winbery and Wallace**

# CASES

| Function | Key Concepts | N.T. Example | *B&W | **Wall |
|---|---|---|---|---|
| **A. NOMINATIVE (Designation)** | | | | |
| 1. Subject nom. | Usual subject | Jn.1:5; 3:35 | 3 | 38 |
| 2. Predicate nom. | Appositional/ linking verb | 1 Jn.4:8; Jn.1:14 | 4 | 40 |
| 3. Nom. of appelation | Used as proper noun | Jn.13:13; Rev.1:4 | 5 | 61 |
| 4. Independent nom. | Absolute (salutations, titles; no sentence) | Mk.1:1, 3; Mt.1:1; Rev.1:1; Rom.1:7 | 5 | 49 |
| 5. Nom. of exclamation | "Brothers!" | Mk.3:34; Rom.11:33 | 7 | 59 |
| 6. Pendent | Logical, not gram. subj. | Jn.1:12; Rev.3:12 | -- | 51 |
| 7. Apposition | Identity ("namely") | Lk.1:13; Rom.1:1 | 7 | 48 |
| **B. VOCATIVE (Address)** | | | | |
| 1. Direct address | Isolated word | Jn.6:68; Lk.1:3 | 64 | 65 |
| 2. Apposition | Identity ("namely") | Mk.5:7; Ac.13:10 | -- | 70 |
| **C. GENITIVE (Description)** | | | | |
| 1. Description | Characterized, described by | Mk.1:4; Jn.2:16; Rom.13:12 | 8 | 79 |
| | Attributed/attributive | Rom.6:4/6:6; Heb.3:12 | -- | 86, 89 |
| 2. Possession | Ownership/ belonging to | Mt.26:51; Jn.1:12 | 8 | 81 |
| 3. Relationship | Familial/marital | Mt.4:21; Jn.6:71 | 9 | 83 |
| 4. Adverbial | Adverb | | | |
|   a. of time | Kind of time | Mt.24:20; Jn.3:2 | 10 | 122 |
|   b. of measure | Price, value, quantity | Mt.10:29; Ju.11 | 11 | 122 |
|   c. of place | Location | Lk.19:4; 1 Pet.1:1 | 12 | 124 |
|   d. of reference | "With reference to" | Heb.5:13; Jas.1:13 | 14 | 127 |
|   e. of association | "With" (συν) | Rom.8:17; Mt.23:30 | -- | 128 |
| 5. Producer/product | Gen produces/is product | Eph.4:3; Phil.4:7/Rom.15:13, 33 | -- | 104, 6 |
| 6. With nouns of action | | | | |
|   a. Subjective | Gen. produces action | Rom.8:35; 16:25 | 15 | 113 |
|   b. Objective | Gen. receives action | 1 Cor.1:6; Mt.12:31 | 15 | 116 |
|   c. Plenary | Both sub and obj | 2 Cor.5:14? Rev.1:1? | -- | 119 |
| 7. Apposition (in, of) | Identity; content; definition; material ("namely") | Rom.4:11; Jn.2:21 | 16 | 95 |
| 8. Partitive | Whole of which a part | Rev.8:7; Mk.6:23; Col.1:15 | 30 | 84 |
| 9. Absolute | Gram. unconnected | Mt.2:1; Mk.9:28 | 17 | 127 |
| 10. Advantage, purpose, dest. | On behalf of; for | Col.4:3; Ac.4:9; Gal. 2:7 18 | 100 | -- |
| 11. Subordination | Dominion ("over") | Mt.9:34; Mk.15:32 | -- | 103 |
| 12. Direct object | With verbs of sense, emotion, sharing, desiring, ruling, buying, accusing | Lk.15:25; Heb.2:14 | 20 | 131 |
| 13. With adjs. advs. nouns | Completes sense | Rom.1:32; Phil.1:27; Mt.26:66 | -- | 134 |
| 14. With prepositions | δια, επι, κατα, μετα, περι, προς, υπερ | | 60-62 | 136 |
| **D. ABLATIVE (Separation)** | | | | |
| 1. Separation | Separation | Ac.27:43; Eph.2:12 | 21 | 107 |
| 2. Source | (Source) from | Ac.1:4; Rom.15:4 | 23 | 109 |
| 3. Agency | Personal | Mt.25:34; Rom.1:7 | 24 | 126 |
| 4. Means | Impersonal | 1 Cor.2:13; Rom.4:11 | 26 | 125 |
| 5. Comparison | "than" | Mt.3:11; 1 Jn.3:20 | 27 | 110 |
| 6. Direct object | Verbs of ceasing, missing, lacking, despairing, comparing | | -- | 131 |

| | | | * | ** |
|---|---|---|---|---|
| 7. Apposition | Identity ("namely") | | -- | 94 |
| 8. With prepositions | αντι, απο, δια, εκ, κατα, αρα, περι, προ, υπο | | 60-62 | 136 |

**E. DATIVE (Interest)**

| | | | * | ** |
|---|---|---|---|---|
| 1. Indirect object | "To, for whom" | Mt.13:13; 18:26 | 32 | 140 |
| 2. Advantage, disadvan. (ethical) | "For" / "Against" | 2 Cor.2:1; Rev.21:2 Mt.23:31 | 33 | 142 |
| 3. Possession | Ownership | Jn.1:6; Lk.1:7 | 35 | 149 |
| 4. Reference (respect) | "With reference to" | Rom.8:12; 6:2 | 36 | 144 |
| 5. Direct object | Verbs of serving, pleasing, helping, believing, worshiping, etc. | Rom.7:25; Jn.3:36 | 37 | 171 |
| 6. Apposition | Identity ("namely") | | -- | 152 |
| 7. With prepositions | εν, επι | | 60-62 | 175 |

**F. LOCATIVE (Position)**

| | | | * | ** |
|---|---|---|---|---|
| 1. Place | Spatial (literal) | Mk.3:34; Ac.5:31 | 38 | 153 |
| 2. Time | Point of time | Lk.24:1; Mt.20:19 | 39 | 155 |
| 3. Sphere | Logical; figurative | 1 Cor.14:20; Mt.5:3 | 40 | 153 |
| 4. Apposition | Identity ("namely") | | -- | 152 |
| 5. With prepositions | εν, επι, παρα, προς | | 60-62 | 175 |

**G. INSTRUMENTAL (Means)**

| | | | * | ** |
|---|---|---|---|---|
| 1. Means | Impersonal | Mk.5:4; Lk.6:1 | 42 | 162 |
| 2. Cause | "Because" Means and reason External-internal | Rom.11:30; Lk.15:17 | 43 | 167 |
| 3. Manner | How | 1 Cor.10:30; 11:5; Ac.11:23 | 44 | 161 |
| 4. Measure | Interval of time, degree | Lk.8:27; Rom.16:25 | 45 | 166 |
| 5. Association (comit. dat.) | Second person in accompany; dir. obj. | Rom.11:2; 1 Cor.4:8 | 47 | 159 |
| 6. Agency | Personal means | Lk.23:15; Gal.5:18 | 48 | 163 |
| 7. Apposition | Identity ("namely") | | -- | 152 |
| 8. With prepositions | εν, επι, παρα, συν | | 60-62 | 175 |

**H. ACCUSATIVE (Limitation)**

| | | | * | ** |
|---|---|---|---|---|
| 1. Direct object | Receives action | Mt.4:21; Jn.8:46 | 49 | 179 |
| 2. Cognate | Same root, idea | Mk.4:41; 1 Pet.5:2 | 50 | 189 |
| 3. Double | | | | |
|   a. Personal & impersonal | "Teach, ask, clothe" | Heb.5:12; Jn.14:26 | 51 | 181 |
|   b. Direct & obj. complem. | "Call, elect, have" | Ac.13:5; Jn.15:15 | 51 | 182 |
| 4. Adverbial | Adverb, modifies verb | | | |
|   a. Measure | Extent of time/space | Mt.20:6; Jn.6:19 | 52 | 201 |
|   b. Manner | "How", "with" | Lk.16:19; Mt.10:8 | 55 | 200 |
|   c. Reference, respect | "With ref. to" | Jn.6:10; Rom.10:5 | 55 | 203 |
| 5. Sub. of infinitive | (cf. acc. of ref.) | Lk.18:16; 1 Co.10:13; He.5:12 | 55-6 | 192 |
| 6. With oaths | "By____" (swearing) | Ac.19:13; 1 Thes. 5:27 | 57 | 204 |
| 7. Absolute | Independent (rare) | Ac.26:3; Eph.1:18 | 58 | 198 |
| 8. Apposition | Identity ("namely") | | -- | 198 |
| 9. With prepositions | ανα, δια, εις, επι, κατα, μετα, παρα, περι, προς, υπερ, υπο | | 60-62 | 205 |

*Brooks, James A. and Winbery, Carlton L. *Syntax of New Testament Greek*. Washington: University Press of America, 1979.
**Wallace, Daniel B. *Greek Grammar Beyond the Basics*. Grand Rapids: Zondervan, 1996.

# PREPOSITIONS

## I.  DEFINITIONS AND DISTINCTIVES

   A.  An adverb specialized to define a case usage.

   B.  A word joined to, and usually placed before, a noun or pronoun to show the relation of a noun to something else.

   C.  The resulting preposition-noun phrase is equivalent to an adjective or an adverb.

   D.  Proper prepositions may be compounded with verbs, not improper prepositions.

   E.  Meaning is determined by the case idea, meaning of the preposition, and context

## II.  ADVERBIAL PREPOSITIONS=IMPROPER PREPOSITIONS (42)

--all are used with the genitive or ablative case except αμα (instru.) and εγγυς (often also with the dative).

   A.  Improper Prepositions Are Used Only With Cases (cannot be compounded with verbs).

      1. ανευ                          4. μεχρι
      2. ενεκα, ενεκεν                  5. αχρι
      3. εως

   B.  Prepositional Adverbs May Be Used Without Cases.

      1. αμα          5. εναντιον      9. κυκλοθεν      13. οψε
      2. εγγυς         6. εντος        10. λαθρα        14. περαν
      3. εσω          7. ενωπιον       11. μεταξυ       15. πλην
      4. εκτος         8. εξω          12. οπισθεν      16. χαριν
      17. χωρις

   C.  Proper Prepositions Are Combined With Adverbs.

      1. εναντι                        3. επανω
      2. εμπροσθεν                     4. υποκατω

   D.  Biblical Circumlocutions By Means Of Nouns With The Genitive

      1. προσωπον (w. απο)             4. ονομα (εις το ονομα)
      2. χειρ (w. δια)                 5. μεσον (ανα μεσον)
      3. στομα (w. δια)

## III. PREPOSITIONAL PHRASES
### A. Conjunctions

1. αχρι ου – until   Lk. 21:24

2. αφ ου – since  Rv. 16:18

3. ανθ ων – because  Lk. 12:3

4. εφ ω – because  Rm. 5:12

5. εφ οσον – inasmuch as (Mt. 25:40), as long as (Mt. 9:15)

6. καθ οσον – inasmuch as, since – Heb. 3:3; 9:27

7. δια τι – why  Mat. 21:25

8. εις τι – why  Mt. 14:31

9. εν ω – while  Lk. 5:34

### B. Adverbs

1. απο μερους – in part –  2 Co. 1:14

2. απο ποτε – from that time on –  Mt. 4:17

3. απ αρτι – henceforth –  Mt. 23:29

4. δια παντος – always --  Mt. 18:10

5. εις το παντελες – completely --  Heb. 7:25

6. εις το παλιν – again --  2 Co. 13:13

7. εις τον αιωνα – forever --  Jn. 6:51

8. εν ταχει – quickly --  Ac. 12:7

9. εν τω μεταξυ – meanwhile --  Jn. 4:31

10. εν αληθεια – sincerely, genuinely --  2 Jn. 1; 3 Jn. 1

11. επ ευλογιαις – bountifully --  2 Co. 9:6

12. κατ ιδιαν – privately --  Ac. 23:19

13. κατ αγνοιαν – ignorantly --  Ac. 3:17

## IV.  PROPER PREPOSITIONS

| PREP | ROOT IDEA | CASE | FUNCTION | MEANINGS |
|------|-----------|------|----------|----------|
| 1. ανα | up | acc | adv. meas. | up, in, back, again, by; each (distrib.) |
| 2. αντι | face to face | abl | cause, exchange substitution | because, of<br>in exchange for, instead of, against, for instead of, in place of |
| 3. απο | off away from | abl | separation/source agency/cause partitive | from/from<br>by/because of, for<br>from, of |
| 4. δια | two | gen<br>abl<br>acc | adv. time/place agency/means cause/relation | through, after/through<br>by/by, through<br>because, for/for the benefit, sake |
| 5. εις | within, in | acc | adv. meas/manner refer purpose/result cause/relation predicate spatial temporal/advantage | unto, for, to, among, into/in<br>with refer. to, about<br>for, for purpose of/result in; so that<br>because of/for, against<br>as, to be<br>into, toward, in<br>for, throughout/for |
| 6. εκ | out of, from within | abl | separation/source means/cause temporal partitive | out of, away, from/from<br>by means of/ because of, result of<br>from<br>of |
| 7. εν | within | dat (?)<br><br><br>loc<br>instr | indir. obj./advan. disadv./refer dir. obj.<br>place/time/sphere means/cause manner/measure assoc./agency possession standard (=meas?) | to/for<br>with, from/about, with ref. to<br>[dir. obj.]<br>in, on, among/at, while/in, within<br>with, by/because of<br>in, with/amounting to, - fold<br>with/by<br>with<br>according to |
| 8. επι | upon | gen<br>dat<br><br>loc<br>instr(?) | adv. time/place/cause indir. obj./refer adv./disadv.<br>place/time/sphere cause | during, at by/on, upon/on basis of<br>to/about<br>to, for/against, upon<br>on, at, upon, over, before/at/in<br>because of; on  basis of |

|        |            | acc        | adv. meas./relat.<br>spatial/temporal | upon, for, on, over/upon, against<br>on, upon, against/for |
|--------|------------|------------|---------------------------------------|-----------------------------------------------------------|
| 9. κατα | down | gen<br>abl<br>acc | place/oaths<br>source/opposition<br>adv. refer/possess.<br>standard/spatial<br>temporal/purpose | throughout, upon/by<br>down from/against (or gen.?)<br>along, at, one (dist.)/of<br>in accordance with/along, at<br>at/for the purpose of |
| 10. μετα | in midst of | gen<br>acc | assoc./atten.cir.<br>adv. measure (temp.,<br>spatial) | with/with, among, on, to<br>after, behind |
| 11. παρα | beside | abl<br>loc<br>instr(?)<br>acc | source/agency<br>place/sphere<br>assoc.<br>adv. meas. (spatial)<br>compar./relation<br>(opposition) | from/by<br>beside, with, before, near/with in<br>with, in presence of?<br>beside, along<br>...than, beyond/against, contrary to |
| 12. περι | around | gen<br>abl(?)<br>acc | refer./advant.<br>purpose<br>adv. meas. (spatial,<br>temporal)/reference | for, about, concerning/for, in behalf of<br>for the purpose of, to...<br>around, about, near<br>/with refer. to, with |
| 13. προ | before | abl | separation/rank<br>temp., spatial | before/above (above all)<br>before |
| 14. προς | near,<br>facing | gen<br>loc<br>acc | advantage (1x)<br>place (6x)<br>adv. meas.(spat, tem)<br>reference<br>purpose/comparison<br>/result<br>relationship<br>(opposition) | in the interest of, for (Ac. 37:34)<br>at, on, near, by<br>with, for, by means of (?)<br>w. refer. to, in accord with<br>so that, for purpose of, to/to compare<br>with/with the result of<br>with, against, to, at |
| 15. συν | together with | instr | meas./assoc. | besides, in addition to/with<br>together with |
| 16. υπερ | over | gen<br><br><br>acc | adv, refer.<br>advantage<br>substitution<br>comparison<br>/spatial | about, as for, concerning<br>for, for the sake of, in behalf of,<br>instead of (substit.)<br>more than, greater than, beyond,<br>  above, over/above, over |
| 17. υπο | under | abl<br>acc | agency/means<br>adv. measure<br>(spatial)<br>subordination | by (direct) /by (impersonal)<br>under, about<br><br>under |

# PRONOUNS

## I. DEFINITION

    A.   A pronoun sets forth the relation of a subject or object to the speaker.

    B.   A pronoun indicates but does not name the speaker.

    C.   Deictic pronouns point out, marking an object by its position in respect to the speaker; anaphoric pronouns refer to substantives, denoting an object already mentioned or known.

    D.   Pronouns stand for, are in the place of, are instead of, a noun; hence they are used as nouns are used (similar syntax).

    E.   Pronouns prevent the monotony which repetition of nouns world cause.

## II. KINDS  (see B & W, 80; Wall., 315-354; charts, 320, 354)

    A.  **Personal** (deictic):  εγω, ημεις, συ, υμεις; no third person
        1.   The nominative is used for emphasis.
        2.   The oblique cases are used as possessive, reflexive (rare) pronouns.

    B.  **Possessive (=adjective):**  εμος, ημετερος; σος, υμετερος; ο, η, το; ιδιος

    C.  **Intensive** (adj. and pron.):  αυτος
        1.   An adjective and pronoun
            a.   intensive adjective pronoun ("self") (predicate use)
            b.   adjective pronoun with the article ("same") (attributive use)
            c.   personal pronoun of third person in oblique cases ("him, her, it, them")
            d.   also used as possessive and demonstrative pronoun ("very, that")
        2.   Emphasizes identity

    D.  **Reflexive:**  εμαυτου, σεατου, εαυτου; εαυτων; ιδιος
        1.   Action is referred back to is own subject.
        2.   The oblique case of a personal pronoun may be so used.

    E.  **Reciprocal:**  αλληλων
        1.   It expresses an interchange of action.
        2.   Also a reflexive pronoun and the middle voice can be so used.

    F.  **Demonstrative:**  ουτος, εκεινος; ο; ος; αυτος; οδε, ηδε, τοδε
        1.   They are regularly placed in predicate position.
        2.   They are used substantively or adjectivally.
        3.   They are deictic unless without article (then anaphoric).
        4.   Sometimes ο μεν, ο δε; ος μεν, ος δε

    G.  **Relative** (anaphoric):  ος, οστις, οσος οιος, οποιος, ηλικος
        1.   Gender and number are determined by antecedent.
        2.   Case is determined by the pronoun's function in its own clause.
        3.   Exceptions to case form are due to attraction (direct or indirect), yet function remains.

4.    Sometimes the antecedent is omitted.

H. **Interrogative:** τις, τι; ποσος (quantity), ποιος (quality), πηλικος (quantity)
     ποταπος, ποτερος
     1.    Used substantively (τις) or adjectively (τις ανηρ)
     2.    Used in direct and in indirect questions
     3.    Used adverbially ("why"); for exclamation; as relative ("what, that which");
           alternatively

I. **Indefinite:** τις, τι; εις . . . εις; πας
     1.    Used substantively ("some one") and adjectively ("some, any, certain")
     2.    Used emphatically ("someone"), numerically; alternatively

J. **Distributive (alternative):** αλληλων, αμφοτεροι, εκαστος; αλλος, ετερος
     (adjective pronouns)

K. **Negative alternative:** ουδεις, μηδεις, ουτις, μητις; ου with πας

L. **Correlative:** τοιουτος ("such") ---οιος, οποιος, ως, τοιοσδε ("such");
     τοσουτος ("so much")---οσος; τηλικουτος ("so great")

# THE ARTICLE

## I. DEFINITIONS AND DISTINCTIVES

A. The basic function is to point out, identify, limit, make definite, define, draw attention to.
   1. Substantives with the article generally are definite or generic; those without the article are indefinite or qualitative.
   2. Presence of the article emphasizes identity, the absence of the article quality.

B. The article is anaphoric not deictic, hence a pointer to what is already there.

C. The article distinguishes individuals, classes, and qualities.

D. The article may be used as a pronoun: demonstrative, alternative (μεν . . . δε), relative, or possessive.

E. The article was originally a demonstrative weakened to the article or strengthened to the relative.

F. Definiteness may be accomplished by the article, use of prepositions, possessive and demonstrative pronouns, and the genitive case.

G. The article may be in the attributive or predicate position with respect to an adjective, or be repeated.

## II. USES (see B & W, 73-79; Wallace, with charts, 255-290)

A. **Identify:** to identify or denote persons or things: το ορος (Mt. 5:1)

B. **Monadic:** to indicate that a substantive is unique: τον κοσμον (Jn. 3:16)

C. **Anaphoric:** to denote previous reference: τους μαγους (Mt. 2:7)

D. **Abstract:** to distinguish one quality from another: η αγαπη (1 Cor. 13:4)
   1. It objectifies or personifies an abstract noun.
   2. It is usually not translated.

E. **Proper name:** to emphasize a proper name (occasional): τον θεον (Ac. 15:19)

F. **Generic:** to distinguish one class or group from another; to show something to be typical or representative of a class or group (translated often as indefinite or as plural): ο εθνικος (Mt. 18:17)

G. **Granville-Sharp rule:** to indicate that substantives connected by και have a special relationship (see Wall., 270-90):

τou μεγαλou Θεou και σωτηρος ημων Ιησou χριστou (Titus 2:13; cf. Jn. 20:17; 2 Cor.1:3; 1 Thes. 3:2; Heb. 12:2; 2 Pet. 1:1, 11; 2:20; 3:18; Rev. 1:9)

H. **Pronomial**
   1. Demonstrative ("this, that; these those"): οι (Heb. 13:24)
   2. Personal ("he, she, they"—nominative case): o (Mt. 13:29)
   3. Alternative: o μεν, o δε; οι μεν, οι δε ("one...another"; "some...others") (1 Cor. 7:7)
   4. Possessive: τον αδελφον (2 Cor. 8:18)
   5. Relative (repetition of the article in a phrase modifying an articular substantive): πιστει τη (1 Tim. 3:13)

I. **Colwell's rule:** to distinguish the subject nominative (articular) from the predicate nominative(anarthrous) in a sentence having a linking verb (cf. Wall., 256-270):

o θεος αγαπη εστιν (1 John 4:8; Mk. 15:36; cf. Jn. 1:1: θεος ην o λογος)

J. **Functional (Bracket use):** To indicate the grammatical function or relationships of indeclinable nouns, participles, infinitives, prepositional phrases, adjectival clauses and modifiers (usually untranslated). The article is used with parts of speech other than a noun: τον απο Ναζαρετ (Jn. 1:45); των δυο (Ac. 1:24);

το της δοξης και το του θεου πνευμα (1 Peter 4:14); το ανεβη (Eph. 4:9).

K. **Substitutional:** to take the place of a noun, when it stands with words or phrases which modify the omitted noun: τα εν τω κοσμω (I John 2:15)

# TENSE (Aspect, Aktionsart)

| Function | Key Concepts | N.T. Example | B&W | Wall |
|----------|--------------|--------------|-----|------|
| **A. PRESENT (Linear)** | | | | |
| 1. Descriptive | Pictorial | Mt.8:25; Jn.5:7 | 84 | 518 |
| 2. Durative | Progressive (adv.) | Lk.13:7; Jn.15:27 | 84 | 519 |
| 3. Iterative (cf. customary) | Repeated action | Rom.8:36; 1 Cor.15:31 | 85 | 520-1 |
| 4. Tendential (conative) | Proposed, attempted "try, attempt" | Gal.5:4; Jn.10:32 | 86 | 534 |
| 5. Gnomic | Universal truth | Mt. 7:17; 2 Cor.9:7 | 86 | 523 |
| 6. Historical (dram.) | Past as present | Mt.3:1; Jn.1:29 | 87 | 526 |
| 7. Futuristic | Fut. as present | Jn.14:3; Mt.27:63 | 88 | 535 |
| 8. Aoristic | Punctiliar | Mk.2:5; Ac.16:18 | 89 | 517 |
| 9. Perfective action | Existing results | Lk.15:27; Gal.1:6 | 89 | 532 |
| **B. IMPERFECT (Linear Past)** | | | | |
| 1. Descriptive | Pictorial | Gal.1:13; Mk.12:41 | 91 | 543 |
| 2. Durative | Progressive | Lk.2:49; 1 Cor. 3:6 | 91 | -- |
| 3. Iterative (cf. customary) | "Kept on, used to" | Mk.15:6; Ac.3:2 | 93 | 546-8 |
| 4. Tendential (conative) | "We're going to, trying to" | Mt.3:14; Lk.1:59 | 93 | 550 |
| 5. Voluntative | Potential; a wish | Rom.9:3; Gal.4:20 | 94 | 550 |
| 6. Inceptive (incho.) | "Began" | Mk.5:32; Ac.3:8 | 95 | 544 |
| **C. FUTURE (Punctiliar)** | | | | |
| 1. Predictive | Future event, state | Ac.2:19; Jn.14:26 | 95 | 568 |
| 2. Progressive | "Keep on" | Rom.6:2; Phil.1:18 | 96 | -- |
| 3. Imperative | "You shall" (cohort) | Mt.1:21; 5:21 | 97 | 569 |
| 4. Deliberative | Rhetorical or real question | Rom.3:6; Mt.11:16 Rom.6:2 | 97 | 570 |
| 5. Gnomic | Universal (few) | Gal.6:5; Rom.5:7 | 98 | 571 |
| **D. AORIST (Punctiliar)** | | | | |
| 1. Constative | Action in entirety | Mt.8:3; Heb.11:13 | 99 | 557 |
| 2. Ingressive | Entrance into state or condition | Ac.15:12; Jn.1:14 | 99 | 558 |
| 3. Culminative | Results, completion of action | Lk.1:1, Ac.5:4 | 100 | 559 |
| 4. Gnomic | Universal | Lk.7:35; Jas.1:11 | 101 | 562 |
| 5. Epistolary | Future as fact (reader's perspect.) | Ac.23:30; Col.4:8 | 102 | 562 |
| 6. Dramatic | Present as past | Mt.3:17; 9:18 | 102 | 564 |
| 7. Proleptic | Future as fact | Jn.15:8; Gal.5:4 | 103 | 563 |

Left-margin bracket annotations for section A. PRESENT:
- linear action (conative) — groups items 1–4
- punct. (unlim.) action — groups items 5–8
- perfect. — groups item 9

## E.  PERFECT (Complete)

| | | | | |
|---|---|---|---|---|
| 1. Intensive | Existing state (cf. present) | Lk.24:46; Jas.1:6 | 104 | 574 |
| 2. Consummative | Past, completed action | Ac.5:28; Rom.5:5 | 105 | 577 |
| 3. Iterative | Repeated action (cf. consum. perfect) | Jn.1:18; 5:37 | 105 | -- |
| 4. Dramatic | Vivid intensive perfect | Jn.1:15; Rev.5:7 | 106 | 578 |
| 5. Gnomic ? | Universal | 1 Cor.7:39; Jn.3:18 | 107 | 580 |
| 6. Aoristic ? | No result | Jn.12:29; 2 Cor.2:13 | 107 | 578 |

## F.  PLUPERFECT (Past Perfect)

| | | | | |
|---|---|---|---|---|
| 1. Intensive | Abiding results | Lk.4:41; Jn.18:16 | 108 | 584 |
| 2. Consummative | Completed action | Lk.8:2; Ac.9:21 | 109 | 585 |

# VOICE (Relates Subject to Verb)

| Function | Key Concepts | N.T. Example | B&W | Wall |
|---|---|---|---|---|
| **A.  ACTIVE  (Subject Produces Action)** | | | | |
| 1. Simple | Subj. produces action | Lk.22;54; 1 Cor.3:6 | 110 | 411 |
| 2. Causative | Subj. causes action | 1 Cor. 3:6; Ac. 13:19 | 110 | 411 |
| 3. Stative | Equative verb or idea | Jn.1:1; 1 Cor.13:4 | -- | 412 |
| **B.  MIDDLE  (Subject Participates)** | | | | |
| 1. Direct | Reflexive | Mk.7:4; Mt.27:5 | 111 | 416 |
| 2. Indirect | Intensive | 1 Cor.13:8; 2 Tim.4:15 | 111 | 419 |
| 3. Permissive | "Permit; cause" | Lk.2:4,5; 1 Cor.6:7 | 112 | 425 |
| 4. Reciprocal | Plural sub. | Mt.26:4; Jn.9:22 | 113 | 427 |
| 5. Deponent | Mid form, act meaning | | -- | 428 |
| **C.  PASSIVE  (Subject Acted Upon)** | | | | |
| 1. Direct | Orig. agent (cf. ὑπο) | Ac.22:30; Mt.10:22 | 103 | 433 |
| 2. Intermediate | Medium  (cf. διά) | Jn.1:3; Mt.1:22 | -- | 433 |
| 3. Impersonal | Instrument (cf. εν, εκ) | Eph.2:8; Mt.3:12 | -- | 434 |

## MOOD  (Manner of Affirmation; Relation to Reality)

| | | | | |
|---|---|---|---|---|
| **A.  INDICATIVE  (Affirms Reality)** | | | | |
| 1. Declarative | States fact (also 1$^{st}$ class cond) | Eph.4:1; Jn.1:1 | 114 | 449 |
| 2. Interrogative | Question | Mt.16:13; Mk.1:24 | 115 | 449 |
| 3. Potential | Contingency | | | |
|    a. Cohortative | Command (fut.) | Lk.1:13; Jas.2:8 | 115 | 451 |
|    b. Obligation | Necessity, possibility | Mt.25:27; Ac.17:29 | 116 | 451 |
|    c. Impulse | Wish | Ac.25:22; Gal.5:12 | 116 | 451 |
|    d. Condition | 2$^{nd}$ class condition | Ac. 26:32; Lk.7:39 | 117 | 450 |
| **B.  SUBJUNCTIVE  (Probability)** | | | | |
| 1. Hortatory | "Let us" | Heb.12:1; 1 Jn.4:7 | 118 | 464 |
| 2. Prohibitive | "Don't ever" | Mt.6:34; Jn.3:7 | 118 | 469 |
| 3. Deliberative | Non-factual question | Mk.12:14; Lk.3:10 | 119 | 465 |
| 4. Emphatic negation | "Never" (ου μη) | Mt.5:20; Lk.6:37 | 119 | 468 |
| 5. Potential | Subordinate clauses (various) | Jn.1:7; Rom.7:2 | 120 | 469 |
| **C.  OPTATIVE  (Possibility)** | | | | |
| 1. Voluntative | Wish, prayer | Ac.8:20; 1 Pet.1:2 | 124 | 481 |
| 2. Potential | Futuristic; 4$^{th}$ class apodosis | Lk.1:62; Ac.8:31 | 125 | 483 |
| 3. Deliberative (oblique) | Indirect question | Lk.1:29; 22:23 | 125 | 483 |
| 4. Conditional | 4$^{th}$ class condition | 1 Pet.3:14; 3:17 | 126 | 484 |
| **D.  IMPERATIVE  (Command)** | | | | |
| 1. Command | Positive demand | Mt.5:44; 6:6 | 127 | 485 |
| 2. Prohibition | "Stop" | 1 Cor.6:9; Rom. 6:12 | 127 | 487 |
| 3. Entreaty | Request ("please") | Mk.9:22; Mt.6:13 | 128 | 487 |
| 4. Permission | Consent given | Mt.8:32; 23:32 | 128 | 488 |
| 5. Condition? | Implied | Jn.2:19; Jas.4:7-8 | 129 | 492 |
| 6. Concession? | Implied | Eph.4:26; Jn.7:52 | 129 | -- |

# INFINITIVES (Verbal Nouns)

| Function | Key Concepts | N.T. Example | B&W | Wall |
|---|---|---|---|---|
| **A.  VERBAL (Adverbial)** | | | | |
| 1.  Purpose | Aim, design | Mt.5;17; Lk.2:22 | 133 | 590 |
| 2.  Result | Result of action | Ac.5:3; Rom.7:3 | 135 | 592 |
| 3.  Time | Relative to verb | | | |
|    a. Antecedent | "Before" (πριν) | Jn.4:49; Mk.14:30 | 136 | 594 |
|    b. Contemporaneous | "While" (εν τω) | Lk.1:21; Mt.13:4 | 136 | 595 |
|    c. Subsequent | "After" (μετα) | Lk.12:5; Ac.1:3 | 137 | 596 |
|    d. Future | "Until" (εως) | Ac.8:40 | 137 | -- |
| 4.  Cause | "Because" (δια) | Mt.13:6; Jas.4:2 | 138 | 596 |
| 5.  Means (rare) | How? (εν τω) | Ac.3:26; 4:29-30 | -- | 597 |
| 6.  Command | Imperatival | Phil.3:16; Rom12:15 | 138 | 608 |
| 7.  Absolute | Greetings | Ac.15:23; Jas.1:1 | 139 | 608 |
| | | | | |
| **B.  SUBSTANTIVAL (Noun, Adjective)** | | | | |
| 1.  Subject | Subject of verb | Mt.3:15; Phil.1:21 | 139 | 600 |
| 2.  Object | | | | |
|    a. Direct | Object of verb | Ac.25:11; 2 Cor.8:11 | 140 | 601 |
|    b. Indirect Discourse | Verb of saying, etc. | Mk.12:18; Jn.12:29 | 140 | 603 |
|    c. Complementary | Completes verb | Heb.7:25; Lk.21:36 | 140 | 598 |
| 3.  Modifier | | | | |
|    a. Of substantives | As adj.; or apposition | Mt.3:14; Jas.1:27 | 141 | 606 |
|    b. Of verbs? | Epexegetical | Rom.1:24; 1:28 | 142 | 607 |

# PARTICIPLES (Verbal Adjectives)

| Function | Key Concepts | N.T. Example | B&W | Wall |
|---|---|---|---|---|
| **A.  ADJECTIVAL (As Adjective or Noun)** | | | | |
| 1.  Attributive | Modifies noun | Phil.4:7; Ac.10:1 | 143 | 617 |
| 2.  Substantival | As a noun | Mt.10:37; Phil.3:17 | 144 | 619 |
| 3.  Predicative | Linking verb | | | |
|    a. Predicate adj. | Additional assertion | Gal.1:22; Rev.1:18 | 144 | 618 |
|    b. Periphrastic | Completes verb | Lk.11:14; 20:6 | 144 | 647 |
| | | | | |
| **B.  ADVERBIAL (As Adverb)** | | | | |
| 1.  Temporal | Relative term ("when") | Rom.4:10; 2 Cor.2:13 | 146 | 623 |
| 2.  Telic | Purpose ("in order to") | Ac.3:26; 8:27 | 147 | 635 |
| 3.  Causal | Reason ("because, since") | 1 Tim.4:8; Lk.23:20 | 147 | 631 |
| 4.  Conditional | ("If") | Heb.2:3; Gal.6:9 | 148 | 632 |
| 5.  Concessive | ("Although") | Heb.5:12; Phil.2:6 | 148 | 634 |
| 6.  Instrumental, means | Means ("by") | Mt.6:27; Lk.15:13 | 149 | 628 |
| 7.  Modal, manner | Manner ("by") | Mt.19:22; Lk.1:64 | 150 | 627 |
| 8.  Complementary | Completes verb | Mt.11:1; 6:16 | 150 | 646 |
|    (supplementary) | Indirect discourse | 3 Jn.4; 1 Jn.4:2 | 150 | 645 |
| 9.  Circumstantial, | Incidental ("and"+verb) | Lk.4:15; Mk.1:7 | 151 | 640 |
|    absolute | Noun & ptc. in gen case | Mt.9:18; Rom.7:3 | 151 | 655 |
| 10. Imperatival | Command | Rom.12:9; 1 Pet.3:1 | 152 | 650 |

# CONJUNCTIONS AND CLAUSES

## I. DEFINITIONS AND DISTINCTIONS

    A. Conjunction is a word that connects words, phrases, clauses and sentences.

    B. Conjunctions may have several meanings.

    C. Conjunctions are a kind of particle.

    D. Particles include the following kinds:

        1.   Intensive (or emphatic):
           γε, δη, ει, μην,νη, μεν, περ, τοι, και, ουν, ποτε, ναι,
           που, πως, αμην, αν, μεντοι

        2.  Negative: ου, μη, μη ου, ου μη

        3.  Interrogative: ου, αρα, τις, αρα, γαρ, ουν, τι

        4.  Conjunctions:  (see below)

        5.  Interjections: ιδε, δευρο, ιδου, ουα, ουαι, ω, ως, τι

## II. KINDS OF CONJUNCTIONS

    A.  **Paratactic (coordinate) Conjunctions:**  connect words, phrases or clauses of equal rank.

        1.   Copulative (connective): τε, δε, αλλα, και (as adjunctive, "also"; as ascensive, "even"; as a connective, "and"); ουδε, μηδε, ουτε, μητε

        2.   Adversative (contrastive):
           δε, αλλα, πλην, μεντοι, ομως, και, μεν, ει μη, καιτοι, ουν, καιτοιγε

        3.   Disjunctive: η, ειτε . . . ειτε, ουτε . . . ουτε

           a.  Inferential (illative): αρα, γαρ, ουν, δη, νυν, τοινυν, ωστε

           b.  Causal: γαρ

           c.   Correlative: μεν . . . δε, και . . . και

           d.  Explanatory: γαρ

           e.  Transitional: δε, ουν

B. **Hypotactic (subordinate) Conjunctions:** connect clauses which are subordinate to (dependent on) the rest of the sentence.

1. Causal: οτι, διο, διοτι, ως, διοπερ, καθως, γαρ, επει, επειδη

2. Comparative: ως, καθως, καθοτι, ωσει, ον τροπον, ωσπερ, καθαπερ

3. Conditional: ει, εαν, αν, ειπερ, επει? (cf. Chart, Wall, 689).

4. Concessive: καιπερ, και ει, ει και, εαν και, καν

5. Relative: ος, οστις (and all of the forms of their declensions)

6. Result: ωστε, ινα, ως, οτι, οπως?

7. Purpose: ινα, οπως, μη after verbs of fearing, ως

8. Temporal: οτε, οταν, αχρι, μεχρις, ως, εως, πριν, επει, επειδη

9. Local: οπου, ου, οθεν

10. Declarative: οτι, ινα, ω

III. **FOUR KINDS OF CONSTRUCTIONS OF SUBORDINATE CLAUSES** (cf. Wall, 659)

A. Infinitival: involve an infinitive

B. Participial: involve a participle

C. Conjunctive: introduced by a subordinate conjunction

D. Relative: introduced by a relative pronoun (ος), a relative adjective (οιος, οσος), or a relative adverb (οπου, οτε)

IV. **THREE SYNTACTICAL FUNCTIONS (USES) OF SUBORDINATE CLAUSES** (cf. Wall, 660)

A. Substantival: subect, predicate nominative, direct object, indirect object, indirect discourse, apposition

B. Adjectival: modify a noun, pronoun, or other substantive

C. Adverbial: cause, comparison, concession, condition, complement, location, manner, means, purpose, result, time

www.ingramcontent.com/pod-product-compliance
Lightning Source LLC
Chambersburg PA
CBHW050403110426

42812CB00006BA/1787